...for this book was gathered by Mark Bego in his personal inter-

	—Susan Seidelman	—Reid Rosefelt
...Benitez	—Mark Kamins	—Mark James Brooky
	—Stephen Jon Lewicki	

...ormation was also taken from the following publications:

—Modern Screen	—Rolling Stone
—the New York Post	—Smash Hits
—Newsday	—Star Hits
...ess —Newsweek	—Teen
—Nightlife	—Us
—19	—USA Today
—People	—Video Rock Stars
—Record Mirror	
...nes —Rock Video	

"MADONNA! is the first book that unmasks pop music's newest female phenomenon, and what a fantastic
read it is! Mark Bego has got to be one of the USA's best
pop biographers!''

—Miles White
USA Today

"Mark Bego is a unique writer, who combines a fan's enthusiasm with a reporter's knack for getting a story. Bego
asks the questions you would ask, and delivers his find-
ings in a way that is entertaining and provocative.

—Paul Grein
Billboard

"Bego and Madonna both hail from southeastern Michigan, and spent considerable amount of time living near
each other in the Detroit area. This book—the first full-
length work on Madonna—carries a hometown boy's
pride and enthusiasm for a neighbor who made good.''

—Gary Graff
Detroit Free Press

"By the time I was around five, I knew that I was going
to have a special life!''

—Madonna

"Madonna is destined to become this generation's
Marilyn Monroe!''

—Mark Bego

Also by Mark Bego from Pinnacle Books

MICHAEL!
ON THE ROAD WITH MICHAEL!

ATT
PINNACLE
purchases fo
further deta
Pinnacle Bo

SOURCES: Mate
views with:
—Madonna
—John "Jellybea
—Maripol

Additional factua
—BAM Magazine
—Billboard
—Cash Box
—the Detroit Fre
—The Face
—Glamour
—Harper's Baza
—Interview
—the Los Angele

MADONNA!

First printin

ISBN: 0-52
Can. ISBN

Printed in

PINNACL
1430 Broa
New York

9 8 7 6 5

PINNACLE BOOKS

To two of my best friends:

Jack "Trippy" Cunningham
&
my cat: Martha Vandella!

Acknowledgments:

The author would like to thank the following people:

—Bart Andrews
—Eugen Beer
—John "Jellybean" Benitez
—Eddie Blower
—Michael Bradley
—Mark James Brooky
—J.B. Carmicle
—Rusty Cutchin
—Gareth Davies
—Scott Downie
—Alf Elkington
—Peter Glankoff
—Roger Glazer
—Gary Graff
—Paul Grein
—Ruth Hunter
—Mark Kamins
—Suzan Kressel
—Mark Lasswell
—June Lazerus
—Madonna
—Maripol
—Stephen Jon Lewicki
—Joe Loris
—Kevin McCarrol
—Dede Miller
—Gerri Miller
—Ivy Miller
—Susan Mittelkauf
—Marie Morreale
—Sondra Ordover
—Robin Platzer
—Private Eyes
—Marissa Redanty
—Sherry Robb
—Reid Rosefelt
—David Salidor
—Susan Seidelman
—Star File Photos
—Larry Steinfeld
—Cherry Vanilla
—Miles White
—Jeannie Williams

Contents:

Introduction

1984 WAS A VERY GOOD YEAR for someone from my hometown of Pontiac, Michigan: Madonna Louise Ciccone. She sold three million records and became the fastest rising new star of the decade. Her fame is just beginning. Not only is she a multimillion-selling recording artist, she is also a video star, and with *Desperately Seeking Susan*, a movie star as well! My crystal ball hasn't failed me yet, and I'm certain that Madonna is destined to become one of the biggest stars of the decade.

It started out slowly, but I suddenly found myself caught up in the whole Madonna phenomenon. I had always been impressed with her brilliantly produced records: from "Everybody" and "Burning Up," to "Like a Virgin" and "Material Girl." Disarmed by her soulful siren's voice, I couldn't seem to escape Madonna's spell. I had known record producer John "Jellybean" Benitez for a couple of years, and suddenly he turned out to be Madonna's boyfriend. Then I learned that Madonna had garnered her record contract through a DJ she had met at Danceteria—the same New York club where I used to host and produce rock shows! Then that demo tape Jellybean had played for me two years ago turned out to be Madonna's first major hit: "Holiday"! The next thing I knew, Madonna was making movies, and I was interviewing her for *Modern Screen* magazine. By the time I found out that she grew up in my hometown, I realized that I was hopelessly hooked on Madonna. I had to write this book!

When I interviewed her in October 1984, we both recalled having met before, but neither of us could remember exactly where or when. She turned out to be everything that I had heard about her: part coy sex kitten, part sensitive young artist, part confident businesswoman, and part bratty Catholic girl. She was arrogant, exotic, friendly, charming, funny, spontaneous, and bewitchingly calculating, all at the same time. I was immediately fascinated by her exciting self-confidence and undeniable presence. Madonna is destined to become this generation's Marilyn Monroe. Her hit song "Material Girl" has already become the most accurate anthem of the decade—it defines the mood of the times. When I visited her on the set of her first major movie, *Desperately Seeking Susan*, I immediately recognized the fact that she is one hundred percent professional.

Not everyone in the world is madly in love with Madonna and her admitted aggressiveness. There are those who say that she brazenly dates the men who can best serve her career plans and then dumps them when they cease to prove useful—like a black widow spider. To complete my quest for information about Madonna, I found many people from various phases of her life eager to talk, and I sought them out like a heat-seeking missile. The facts are all here to read; you be the judge.

Personally, I admire Madonna's relentless determination. I can honestly say that I have found her to be one of the most fascinating and candid subjects that I have ever written about. She knows where she's going, and she knows how to get there. She matter-of-factly admits, "From when I was very young, I just knew that being a girl and being charming in a feminine sort of way could get me a lot of things, and I milked it for everything I could!" You can say that again, Madonna.

Is she a gutsy gold-record goddess, or is she just a gold digger? Is she really "like a virgin," or is she just an ambitious "material girl"? Read on. I've got the lowdown on Madonna—a smart cookie who knows that stardom IS a girl's best friend!

—MARK BEGO
February 1985

MADONNA!

The Madonna Phenomenon

SHE BURST LIKE A SKYROCKET into the forefront of the music scene in 1984 with her hit records "Holiday," "Borderline," and "Lucky Star." She began 1985 with her multimillion-selling smash LP and single "Like A Virgin," both across-the-board number-one international hits. Her video performances have created an indelible image of a free-spirited "material girl" of the eighties that has made her a multimedia phenomenon. Now, to top it all off, Madonna has become a movie star!

Her first major film portrayal is the title role of Susan in the offbeat comedy *Desperately Seeking Susan*. She also lensed a small part singing two songs in the movie *Vision Quest*, but it is as the eccentric Susan that Madonna has found screen stardom.

She is a fashion statement on legs, and Madonna's penchant for dozens of black rubber bracelets, crucifixes, amulets, and mismatched earrings has caused a new fashion sensation. Unlike Cyndi Lauper's now-famous thrift shop crinolines and prom gowns, Madonna ties her streaked hair in rags and dons funky designer clothes. Her midriff is almost always bare or thinly covered in netting. Around her waist she often teasingly wears a belt buckle emblazoned with the words "Boy Toy."

Her choreography is fluidly kinetic instead of haphazard—due to years of dance training. While Lauper acts like a New Wave Betty Boop, and Pat Benatar portrays an unobtainable rock-and-roll high priestess, Madonna personifies a combination of street-wise bad-girl waif and superconfident Continental dance diva.

In high school she was a junior varsity cheerleader, and after graduation she turned her back on a University of Michigan scholarship to run away to New York City to become a dancer. She came from a background of theater and dance, picking up polish along the way via an apprenticeship with the Alvin Ailey Dance Company and six months in the fast lane in Paris.

Madonna recalls, "I always had the idea that I wanted to be a performer, but I wasn't sure if I wanted to sing or dance or be an actress or what, so I concentrated on dancing." She instinctively knew that she was meant to find her way to the top, and is quick to admit, "I always acted like a star, even before I was one!"

From 1979 to 1981 she was one of the stars of an experimental low-budget film called *A Certain Sacrifice*. Then she shifted gears and put all her energy into becoming a singer, coming up with a demo tape of a song she had written called "Everybody."

Says Madonna, "Most people think there is something secret or magical to being a singer or writing a song. But you can do whatever you want. You have to throw out all of the rules and all the advice everyone gives you about how to make it—and follow your own vision, if you have one."

With that sense of bravado, she strutted up to the DJ booth of New York rock club Danceteria and asked smitten disk jockey Mark Kamins to toss "Everybody" onto the turntable. Kamins loved the record, produced a new version of it, and garnered a record deal for Madonna with the understanding that he would produce the subsequent album deal, if all went well. When the contracts were signed, Kamins' production deal wasn't on paper.

Reggie Lucas, who had won Grammys for his work with Stephanie Mills, was brought in to finish the debut LP *Madonna*. As the pressing date drew near, Sire Records decided that one particular cut titled "Ain't No Big Deal" was too weak for inclusion on the album, so Madonna enlisted her current boyfriend, John "Jellybean" Benitez, to come up with "Holiday" in two days' time! Madonna's dance hits "Everybody" and "Burning Up" laid the groundwork, but it was "Holiday," which crossed over to spend over six months on the pop-record charts, that made Madonna a star to watch. Then came two consecutive top-ten pop hits: "Borderline" and "Lucky Star."

Backed by her steamy videos of "Burning Up," "Borderline," and "Lucky Star," Madonna's face was all over television. She next filmed performances in two movies and went to work on her second album, titled *Like A Virgin*. After she had completed her first album, she and Jellybean produced two cuts for the film *Vision Quest*, titled "Gambler" and "Crazy For You," and she wrote a song for his debut album, a tune called "Sidewalk Talk," which became a number-one dance hit. But when it came time to choose a producer for *Like A Virgin*, she found that neither Benitez, Kamins, nor Lucas would do. She chose instead to work with Nile Rodgers, who produced such number-one hits as David Bowie's "Let's Dance" and Diana Ross' "Upside Down." Apparently her instincts proved correct, for "Like A Virgin" became a million-selling number-one hit in a matter of weeks!

Says Madonna of her hit-and-run tactics, "Sometimes I feel guilty because I feel like I travel through people. I think that's true of most ambitious, driven people. You take what you can and then move on. If the people can't go with me or move, whether it's a physical move or emotional, I feel sad about that. But that's part of the tragedy of love."

Supported by a lush video that was shot on location in Venice, "Like A Virgin" crystallized the sex kitten image with shades of Brigitte Bardot. For her next video presentation, it was off to Hollywood to cement the Marilyn Monroe correlation by staging her hit "Material Girl" like Monroe's show-stopping movie production number "Diamonds Are A Girl's Best Friend" from *Gentlemen Prefer Blondes*.

Madonna shamelessly admits, "I'd love to be a memorable figure in the history of entertainment, in some sexual comic-tragic way. I'd like to leave the impression that Marilyn Monroe did, to be able to arouse so many different feelings in people."

Director Susan Seidelman, who worked with Madonna in *Desperately Seeking Susan*, sees Madonna as a comic actress à la Carole Lombard. Adds Maripol (pronounced "Mary Paul"), Madonna's French jewelry designer and confidante, "Madonna is a child-woman. She is fun and joyful, but she is also a femme fatale. She is vulnerable—but then she's not that vulnerable. She's not tough exactly, but she'll survive through anything. She's a natural star. She is born to stardom."

"I can be arrogant sometimes," Madonna confesses, "but I never mean it intentionally. I can be really snotty to people, but that's not anything new, really. If people don't see my sense of humor, then I come off as being expensive, but I always endear myself to people when I find their weaknesses and they acknowledge it. It's the people who try to hide everything, and try to make you think they're so cool that I can't stand.

"I'm vulnerable to people who want to rape my soul. You know, like journalists. It's weird, it depends on what kind of mood you're in. Sometimes I'll be doing a photo session with someone that I've done a lot of work with and all of a sudden I feel like they've seen too much and I don't want them to look at me anymore. Usually I'm pretty outgoing and gregarious, but I can be really shy about things sometimes," she says. Defending her tough-as-nails veneer, she adds, "I know I may give that impression, and I am pretty tough now, but it wasn't always that way. The first couple of years in New York were torture for me. The whole place was so intimidating. I didn't know anyone. I had no money. I'd go to Lincoln Center, sit by the fountain, and just cry. I'd write in my little journal and pray to have even one friend. Even in dance school, most of the kids on scholarship were inner-city kids who had a much different temperament than I did. I was kind of off to myself in a little corner. I had been used to being a big fish in the little pond [Michigan], and all of a sudden I was a nobody. I longed for that familiarity and being on top of everything. But never once did it occur to me to go back home—never!''

Well, she's certainly come a long way in a short period of time. At the age of twenty-five, she's gone from dreaming about stardom to comparing fashion tips with Barbra Streisand! *Vision Quest* producer Jon Peters invited Madonna to dinner at La Streisand's, and she really knew she had arrived on the scene. Recalls Madonna, ''It was great. I had dinner at her house, and she was genuinely interested in an exchange as one singer to another. I had this rag tied in my hair the way I do, and she wanted to know everything about the way I dressed, the jewelry I wore, the way I sang, about how I grew up in Detroit.'' Can you imagine it? ''Material Girl'' meets ''Funny Girl'' at dinner? Outrageous!

Not every woman in show business is amused. Gina Schock, a drummer and percussionist for the Go-Go's, snidely remarks, ''People like her give people like us a hard way to go. She doesn't help anybody take women seriously. But you know what? I love the record!''

Madonna couldn't care less. She'd rather be a naughty star than a nice nobody. ''I already knew that people were never going to think of me as a nice girl when I was in the fifth grade,'' she proclaims. ''I don't want anyone to ever forget me. It's not enough to have a few people as friends and a few people patting you on the back. You want everybody to be touched by you, everyone to love you. Put out vibes and you get what you want. I always meet people at certain times in my life who can help me." Still, she adds, "the people I've been with are really shrewd. They weren't going to let me walk all over them—no way!"

What does her music represent? "It's all about escapism," Madonna explains, "to make people forget about the problems of the world. It's just to cheer people up. People go out to dance and get away and forget about their problems, like a holiday, and that's what the music's about—to get together and forget."

However, Madonna never gets lost in her music, and she never, never forgets what she is doing or where she is going. "Romance should be spontaneous, but in my career I'm totally in control," she insists. She is quite determined not to become a rock-and-roll casualty: "I prefer film habits simply because I don't like to sit up all night and party. I like to see the sun shine. And since I was trained as a dancer, I know all about working long hours, taking care of yourself, and getting enough sleep, because you have to look healthy on camera."

She retains a great sense of humor about herself, admitting, "My rock-and-roll fashion image is a contradiction. My two favorite fantasies were always a cross between Nancy Sinatra and a nun!" One could hardly mistake Madonna for a singing nun. When she did a four-page fashion spread for *Harper's Bazaar* recently, the magazine heralded her as possessing "a combination of movie queen glamour and tough-punk sensuality." The spread's internationally famed photographer, Francesco Scavullo, found Madonna's beauty reminiscent of Marlene Dietrich.

"You want it, you find a way to get it," claims Madonna. "I think most people who meet me know that's the kind of person I am. It comes down to doing what you have to do for your career." Well, her career is definitely moving along in high gear. Not only is she a hit in America, she's the darling of the United Kingdom, Australia, Brazil, France, Canada, and South Africa as well! The media blitz has just begun, the cover of *Rolling Stone* in America and the cover of *The Face* in Britain have helped seduce record buyers and moviegoers on both sides of the Atlantic. Videophiles have been kept pacified with Madonna's first videotape, and a second collection is already in the works.

According to Madonna, she wants to do it all. "Three to four years ago, dancing was the most important thing, now it's music. That will lead on to something else—acting. Above all, I want to be an all-around entertainer, and happy. I want to keep on making great records and want to develop as a music artist, but also to get involved in other things as well. I'd like to make more videos and to write music for other people, and then I have a great interest in films."

All this is just the beginning for hyperactive Madonna. She proclaims, "If there were ten rungs on a ladder, I'd say I was on the third rung now. I think I'll always have goals. I can't imagine ever reaching the end and saying, 'That's all I want to do!' "

Madonna is so determined, self-motivated, and aggressive that she makes Joan Collins' character on TV's *Dynasty* look laid back! What is it that makes Madonna tick? To answer this question, I interviewed

John "Jellybean" Benitez, Maripol, Mark Kamins, Susan Seidelman, Madonna, and many more industry insiders, to paint a full portrait of one of the hardest working, sexiest, and most talked-about multimedia stars of the decade. From Motown to Manhattan to the movie screen, here is the whole story behind the magical street-wise bad girl who calls herself "Madonna"!

2

Pontiac, Michigan

CONVERSATION—OCTOBER 8, 1984:

"You know, we're both from Pontiac, Michigan!" Mark Bego commented.

"Really?" Madonna replied. "You know where Featherstone Road is, where the Silverdome is?"

"Yes."

"That used to be woods and trees. I used to play there. They tore it all down."

"Have you been back there?"

"No, my parents moved to Rochester, Michigan."

"Everybody leaves Pontiac," I concluded, having had my writing debut on the *Pontiac Press*.

"If they don't, they're finished!" she said. Having studied dance to the extent that Pontiac had to offer, she knew she had to move on.

Pontiac Motor Corporation, General Motors Truck & Coach, and the Silverdome stadium are the three biggest things in Pontiac, Michigan. After the 1967 race riots in both Detroit and Pontiac, nobody wanted to have much to do with Pontiac. It's a shame, but what was once downtown Pontiac is a mere gray shell of what used to be a bustling city in the twenties and thirties.

Madonna and I never met in Pontiac. I was born there and grew up in the vicinity, and her family moved a few miles north to Rochester. Both of us grew up on Motown music, and we both gravitated to New York City.

"Madonna is my real name," she confirms. "It means a lot of things. It means virgin, mother, mother of earth, someone who is very pure and innocent, but someone who's very strong." It obviously fits the image—and the legend.

Madonna Louise Ciccone was born on August 16, 1959, north of Pontiac, in Bay City, Michigan. ("Industrial—smells like New Jersey, kind of," she laughingly recounts.) The oldest daughter in a large Italian family, Madonna has five brothers and two sisters. When the family moved down to Pontiac, Madonna's father went to work for Chrysler Corporation as an engineer.

"I grew up in Pontiac," Madonna remembers, "and it was during the riots, and all the black people, the black families were coming into the neighborhood, and all the white families were freaking out and moving out. That was during the sixties when all the looting and stuff was going on. We were one of the families that didn't move. I went to the Catholic school there. I had to get bused there from the neighborhood I lived in, and most of the kids that lived down the block went to the local public school. So I'd come home in my uniform, but I didn't hang out with the girls in my school.

"I grew up in a really big family and in an environment where you had to get over it to be heard. I was like the she-devil. My father used to pay us money for the grades we got on our report cards, and he geared me up for being competitive when I was really young," says Madonna.

Then when she was seven years old, something very tragic happened that strengthened her survival instincts. Her mother died of cancer. It was after her mother that Madonna was named, and it was from the experience of her death early in Madonna's life that she decided to become the master of her own fate.

She recalls, "My mother died when I was really young, so I didn't have this image of what feminine girls do or anything. And my father never brought me up to get married and have kids. He actually brought me up to be very goal oriented, to be a lawyer or doctor and study, study, study. We didn't get allowances, but we definitely got rewards for achieving. And I have all these brothers and sisters, so of course I sought out the opportunity to be number one all the time. I got the best grades: straight As! Subsequently, all my brothers and sisters hated me. I was the tattletale of the family. I was the rat fink. I had my father wrapped around my finger. No, no, I mean I was the oldest girl. I had two older brothers, but they would skip classes all the time. They were really bad boys."

Music was always important to Madonna. "They were always playing records, those little portable old 45s that you could carry together like a suitcase. They just stuck them out on their front porch or in their driveways.'' She says about the kids in the neighborhood where she grew up, ''When I was growing up, my older brothers were into hard rock and I hated it. And they would purposely scratch the needle across my pop records, like my 'Incense And Peppermints' record and my Gary Puckett 'Young Girl, Get Out Of My Mind' record, and they would tell me it was trash and say, 'Get that out of here.' Then they'd put on something like Mahavishnu Orchestra.

''From the start I was a very bad girl,'' Madonna says, priding herself on being a naughty Catholic girl. ''I went to three Catholic schools as a child (St. Andrew's, St. Frederick's, and Sacred Heart Academy) with uniforms, and nuns hitting you over the back with staplers. I've always worn crucifixes—I had this thing about nuns and crucifixes. It appeals to me; there's something very mysterious and alluring about it. So I kind of adapted it in my own bastardized way,'' she explains of her religious-jewelry fetish.

''By the time I was around five, I knew that I was going to have a special life. My father was always angry with me. He wanted me to have more humility, more modesty. I was very loud and gregarious and aggressive and a show-off. I'm sure a lot of it stems from insecurity. I had lots of brothers and sisters, and I was constantly fighting for attention after my mother died,'' says Madonna. ''I never got anything easy when I was growing up. My father didn't believe in a lot of leisure. He always felt I should be doing my homework or reading the Bible or meditating in my room. I'm sure he thought deep down inside that when

I was hanging out with my friends, I was doing bad things or getting into trouble.

"I wanted to do everything everybody told me I couldn't do. I had to wear a uniform to school, I couldn't wear makeup, I couldn't wear nylon stockings, I couldn't cut my hair, I couldn't go on dates, I couldn't even go to the movies with my friends. So when I'd go to school, I'd roll up my uniform skirt so it was short. I'd go to the school bathroom and put makeup on and change into nylon stockings I'd brought. I was incredibly flirtatious, and I'd do anything to rebel against my father.

"I had a musical upbringing. I studied piano for a year, but I quit and convinced my father to let me take ballet lessons instead. As I got older, I learned jazz, tap, and modern dance. We held parties in our backyards. Someone would bring a little turntable. We'd pile on a stack of 45s and dance. Every chance to make up a little song-and-dance routine, I took advantage of it, and I always got standing ovations. Finally I decided to devote myself professionally to it. I started taking ballet classes with a really strict ballet teacher—he was very Catholic and disciplined. He's the one who really inspired me. He kept saying, 'You're different,' and 'You're beautiful.' He never said I'd make a great dancer; he just said, 'You're special.' " That's all the encouragement she needed.

"I never had a group of friends in school. I kept to myself and did what I wanted to do. But it bothered me. I think I was lonely in lots of ways. And when I latched on to the dance thing, I was with older and more sophisticated people. I felt really superior. I just felt that all this suffering that I felt for not fitting in was worth it. 'I don't fit in because I don't belong here,' I thought. 'I belong in some SPECIAL world!' ''

Things were changing around her, and Madonna wanted to change too. Her father remarried, the family moved north of Pontiac to Rochester, Michigan, and Madonna began to go to a public high school. Madonna recalls, ''My father's marriage was a surprise to us, because we all thought he was going to marry someone else who looked very much like our mother, and we were rooting for her. My mother looked sorta like Natalie Wood, or that's what I thought she looked like when I was a child. But then suddenly he didn't marry her. I wasn't too fond of my stepmother. She was really gung-ho, very strict, a real disciplinarian. It was hard to accept her as an authority figure and also accept her as being a new number-one female in my father's life. My father wanted us to call her 'Mom,' not her first name. I remember it being really hard for me to get the word 'Mother' out of my mouth. It was really painful. I hated the fact that my mother was taken away, and I'm sure I took a lot of that out on my stepmother.''

Madonna always found something to occupy her time with. In the eighth grade she made her film debut. A classmate had a super-8 camera and shot footage of Madonna frying an egg on her stomach. Yes, even then she knew that the spotlights were calling her!

Rochester Adams High School. No more Catholic schoolgirl uniforms, and a chance to stretch out a bit more and find herself. In December 1984 I met one of Madonna's high school classmates, Mark James Brooky. We talked about Michigan, Adams High School, and a girl that he used to have his eye on: Ma-

donna Ciccone. Brooky loaned me his yearbooks from
high school. It's funny how much you can learn from
those yearbooks. They're like discovering a time capsule. Since I'm a couple of years older than Madonna,
and Adams never played Andover in football, I missed
Madonna as a cheerleader, but those days of pom-
poms and plaid pleated skirts remain alive in the yearbooks.

One page in the 1974 Highlander yearbook shows
off our favorite "material girl" as a junior varsity cheerleader. A legend at the top of the page reads: "Can you
imagine what life at Adams would have been like without our JV cheerleaders? Quieter, for one thing. This
year's JV squad had enough spirit for several teams.
Seven sophomores and one junior inspired the JV
teams through the fall and winter seasons. Both in bas-
ketball and football, these girls showed spirit in even
the darkest moments. Four of these girls were 'veteran' Freshman cheerleaders, and the other four made
their cheering debut this year. Their teacher-sponsor,
Mrs. Pershinske, helped the girls from the beginning,
coaching them as they continuously practiced their
cheering and pom-pom routines. Working as a unit,
the girls were able to show the student body what the
spirit of '75 and '76 really means."

One photo of the JV cheerleaders shows Madonna and the girls meeting with the cheerleaders from
Groves High School. Another shot shows the eight
Adams cheerleaders in pyramidlike formation. On the
top row stands brunette Madonna Ciccone with flow-
ing shoulder-length hair; she's flashing a happy smile.
(See the photo insert in this book.) In the same year-

book are shots of Madonna in the homecoming assembly, making one of her debut dramatic performances.

In the next year's Adams yearbook, we see Madonna with script in hand, rehearsing for the school production of the play *Dark of the Moon* and in a student tutoring program called "Help-A-Kid." During the school year, Adams held what it called "Winter Carnival Week," which included a talent show. Mark Brooky explained to me as he handed me his yearbooks, "There's a picture of her in one of these where she's dancing. She's got a white thing on, and black knickers, and she's dancing. It has a dumb little caption on it. It was a talent show. I think she sang, and it didn't seem like anyone was impressed. She didn't bomb out, but I don't think that anyone was real impressed. We didn't know that she was going to sell a million records!" Sure enough, I found the picture, and there is Madonna doing a dance in the high school gym, wearing black satin knickers, white socks, and a pair of Mary Jane dance shoes. The caption reads: "Honest, it's really me . . . cross my heart!"

"I don't remember her personally well," claims Brooky, "but I remember seeing her go up and down the hall. We used to have a rating system for all the girls, and we had a top ten, all of us guys. I think she got a nine out of a possible ten!"

As I was thumbing through Mark's 1974 yearbook, I found a piece of notebook paper where girl-crazy Brooky stashed his own personal top-ten lists. There under the heading of "Sophomores," scrawled in pencil is "7: Madonna Ciccone." Apparently, Madonna impressed him enough to rank number seven instead of number nine like the rest of his friends.

In her senior class yearbook, Madonna is shown as a member of the Adams Thespian Society, which staged its production of *The Night Thoreau Spent in Jail* that year. Her graduation picture shows her with straight brunette bobbed hair. Her makeup may have been different, but it is unmistakably Madonna.

Brooky isn't in contact with Madonna at all. In fact, it wasn't until "Holiday" began to receive air play that it became clear to him that *that* was one of his classmates. He is currently a production manager at station WKGR in West Palm Beach, Florida. "I didn't even like the song—I kept turning it off! I thought, 'Who's that?' Then my sister sent down a newspaper article from the *Detroit News* or the *Detroit Free Press*. It had her picture there, and said that she graduated from Rochester High School or something like that. My sister didn't know we happened to be in the same high school graduating class!" he recounted to me.

"Do you remember anything else?" I pried in our brief conversation about high school Madonna.

BROOKY: I do remember. The same group of guys who gave her a nine, told me, at least one of them, her reputation was not admirable.

BEGO: You mean she wasn't "like a virgin"?

BROOKY: No. That's the rumor at the time in high school, but you know how those go. At least one or more people in high school told me that.

BEGO: Of course, high school reputations you could never put much money on, because everybody talked big. You don't

remember her wearing any wild jewelry
or anything, do you?

BROOKY: No. As the years progressed there, from
a cheerleader as a sophomore, she
seemed to be more popular. By senior
year, she seemed to be less popular. She
cut her hair and seemed to be more
withdrawn and conservative. And now
she's flying out the other way!

You can say that again! It was apparent that Madonna Ciccone was trying to decide how to escape
from suburban Detroit and find the fame she somehow
knew she was destined for.

After graduating from Rochester Adams High
School in the spring of 1976, it was off to Ann Arbor,
Michigan, to the University of Michigan to study
dance on a scholarship.

According to Madonna, her ballet teacher gave her
"my introduction to glamour and sophistication." She
found out that there was a whole other world out there.
"He used to take me to all the gay discotheques in downtown Detroit. Men were doing poppers and going
crazy. They were all dressed really well and were more
free about themselves than all the blockhead football
players I met in high school. He made me push myself.
He was constantly putting all that stuff about New
York in my ear. I was hesitant and my father and everyone was against it, but he really said, 'Go for it.' "

The University of Michigan is known as a "party
school," so Madonna really got into the swing of
things. "I was a real ham!" she recalls. "I did everything I could to get attention and be the opposite of

everyone else. I'd rip my leotards and wear teeny little safety pins. And I'd run my tights. I could have gone to a nightclub right after class!''

One night in the preppy Ann Arbor disco The Blue Frogge, Madonna spotted a black waiter who looked like he was more fun than the rest of the patrons. "He was real cute," Madonna recalls, "someone all soulful and funky looking you couldn't help but notice. First time in my life I asked a guy to buy me a drink." The man's name was Steve Bray, and at the time he was also the drummer in a local group. Bray showed Madonna the ropes of the music scene and provided her with a more exciting education than the University of Michigan dance department was offering.

Bray remembers, "She wasn't really a musician back then; she was just dancing. She stood out, quite. Her energy was really apparent. What direction she should put that energy in hadn't been settled, but it was definitely there."

According to Madonna, "Those were good days. But I knew that my stay at Michigan was short-term. To me, I was just fine-tuning my technique." When she left for New York City, Madonna left Steve Bray in the dust. She had been at U of M for five semesters; that was enough. "Looking back," says Madonna, "I think that I probably did make him feel kind of bad, but I was really insensitive in those days. I was totally self-absorbed." Look out, New York City!

3

Crossing
the Borderline

IN 1978 MADONNA LEFT Michigan and got on a jet bound for New York City. "It was the first plane ride of my life. I didn't know anyone. I didn't have a place to stay. I had thirty-five dollars in my pocket. I told the taxi driver to take me to the middle of everything. I was let off in Times Square!" she recalls.

Madonna promptly auditioned for a dance scholarship with the Alvin Ailey Dance Theater, won a work/study scholarship, and took classes with the troupe's third-string company. According to Madonna, "I thought I was in a production of *Fame*! Everyone was Hispanic or black, and EVERYONE wanted to be a star!"

Studying with a dance company hardly pays one's rent in New York City, so Madonna decided to serve humanity: at Dunkin' Donuts, that is! "Once I had gotten the scholarship, they put me in their work/study

23

program, and I got the doughnut job. I later found this horrible walk-up in which to live,'' she recounts. ''When my father came to visit, he was mortified—the place was crawling with cockroaches. There were winos in the hallway, and the entire place smelled like stale beer. He couldn't understand how I could give up a scholarship at, in his eyes, this incredible university to come live in a rathole without any money.''

From Alvin Ailey, Madonna became acquainted with Pearl Lange, a former dancing star with the Martha Graham troupe, who was teaching too. Madonna became her assistant. Of Lange's company, she comments, ''It was interesting work. The style is very archaic—angular and dramatic. Painful, dark, and guilt-ridden: very Catholic. I was always an outcast in my ballet classes, the freak. I didn't have long hair pulled back in a bun. Mine was short, and I used to dye it different colors. I wanted to dance in New York, but there weren't many companies that I wanted to work in. The best ones didn't need anyone. Their dancers knew they were with the best and weren't going anywhere. I wasn't willing to wait five years for a break, so I started going to musical-theater auditions.''

During this same time, Madonna met two brothers: Dan and Ed Gilroy. They were both musicians who had rented out an old synagogue in Queens. Another of her acquaintances at this time was French disco singer Patrick Hernandez, who had one notable international record, titled ''Born To Be Alive.'' She had originally auditioned for Hernandez' managers because they were trying to build an act around his record career. They announced to Madonna that they were interested in making her a singing star in her own right. They promised her the moon, and off to Paris flew Madonna!

Madonna explains, "They took me to Paris and gave me everything: a vocal coach, a dance teacher, an apartment, and a chauffeur. Before meeting them, I had been eating out of garbage cans, so to speak. They were like French Mafia, very wealthy and had come into even more money through Patrick. They knew I was talented, but had no idea what to do with me. Living in Paris was like a French movie. They kept telling me I was going to be the next Edith Piaf and dragged me around to show their friends what they had found in the gutters of New York. I felt miserable." Madonna felt like a squashed cabbage leaf and wasn't happy with playing Eliza Doolittle to anyone's Henry Higgins.

She stuck a hole in the balloon and acted like a spoiled brat to get out of the whole scene. "They made me meet rich French boys—I hated them all. We'd go to an exclusive restaurant, and I'd be a brat and refuse to eat. Instead, I demanded money. When they gave it to me, I'd run out and go riding on motorbikes with these low-life Vietnamese boys I knew. It was a great adventure, but I tired of it. I had gotten used to working hard in New York, and feeling my progress. After six months I told them that I was going home to visit. I left everything I had there and never returned. Once again I was forced into the role of *enfant terrible*. All I wanted to do was make trouble because they stuck me in an environment that didn't allow me to be free," says La Madonna.

While she was still in Paris, she would receive letters from Dan Gilroy. "His letters were so funny," says Madonna. "He'd paint a picture of an American flag and write over it, like it was from the President: 'We miss you. You must return to America.' He really made me feel good. He was my saving grace."

After she moved back to New York Madonna refers to the period as "my intensive musical training." She and the brothers Gilroy and an ex-dancer named Angie Smit formed a band they called the Breakfast Club. Madonna recalls, "It was one of the happiest times of my life. I really felt loved. Sometimes I'd write sad songs, and he'd sit there and cry. Very sweet."

While the band was polishing up their repertoire, Madonna was busy on the phone trying to get the group some work. Remembers Dan Gilroy, "She'd be up in the morning, a quick cup of coffee, then right to the phones, calling up everybody—everybody! Everyone from Bleecker Bob's [record store] to potential management. Anything and everything."

Ambitious Madonna decided to dive right in and take control of the group's future. "I was just a lot more goal oriented and commercial minded than they were. I just took over in the sense that I said, 'What do you know? Teach it to me.' I took advantage of the situation. I wanted to know everything they knew, because I knew I could make it work to my benefit. Immediately, when I started working with them, I started thinking record deals, making records and doing shows and stuff like that. And, of course, most of the people you have to deal with are men, and I think I just was naturally more charming to these old businessmen than Dan and Ed Gilroy." She admits, "I was always thinking in my mind, 'I want to be a singer in this group too,' and they didn't need another singer.''

She did get her one chance, and it was the deciding card dealt her. "We played all the Lower East Side hell holes," recounts Madonna. "I convinced them to let me sing a song. It got the best reaction, and they got upset. I wanted to sing more. They said, 'No way.' I said, 'Good-bye!' ''

After one year as one-quarter of the Breakfast Club, Madonna decided to leave Queens and the synagogue and the Gilroy brothers and move back to Manhattan to pursue her own musical career. Dan Gilroy reminisces, "I knew that with that kind of drive and devotion to getting ahead, something had to happen. I missed her very much.''

Determined to strike while the iron was hot, Madonna got on the phone and formed a band. One of the first calls she made was to Michigan, which put her back in touch with Steve Bray. Remembers Bray, "I found out that oddly enough she needed a drummer, so I said, 'Fine, I'll be there next week.' '' Madonna sighs, "He was a lifesaver. I wasn't a good enough musician to be screaming at the band about how badly they were playing.''

The building in which Madonna and Bray used to rehearse was full of musicians trying to get their acts together. Among the other musicians were bands like Nervus Rex, the Dance, and the System. Madonna had a good eye for who was going to accomplish something, and who was not. "I thought they were all lazy," she says, quick to judge. "I felt a lot of affection for them, but I thought that only a handful of people were going to get out of that building to any success.'' The only thing that she was one hundred percent positive about was that she was going to rise to the top or else!

Bray admits, ''I think there was a lot of resentment of someone who's obviously got that special something. There are so many musicians out there, but there are only a few who really have that charisma. The community out there kind of, I think, frowned on her about that. She had trouble making friends. It was like living in a commune, very closed-minded thinking—if you're good in New York, you can get regular jobs at CBGB's or at Danceteria, that's fine, you've made it.''

Madonna and Steve kept changing the name of their band: the Millionaires, Modern Dance, and Emmy. Recalls Ms. Ciccone, ''I wanted just 'Madonna.' Steve thought that was disgusting.''

Continues Bray, ''She was playing really raucous rock and roll, really influenced by the Pretenders and the Police. She used to really belt. If we'd found that right guitar player, I think that's when things would have taken off, but there are so many horrible guitar players in New York, and we seemed to get them all.''

Madonna tells her side of the story by stating, ''I had a band called Emmy when I came across this manager [Camille Barone] who told me to forget all this adolescent-band crap. She hired good studio musicians to work with me. She encouraged me to write my own songs, but we didn't see eye to eye on the direction I was headed. She wanted me to do Pat Benatar-like rock. I was trying for a more funky sound, black stuff. She told me that I couldn't do that because I was a little white girl. I refused to listen. You can't have a manager who wants to exploit your identity if you have a different idea of what your identity is going to be. We split, not too amiably. I'm proud of the fact that I started out as a rhythm-and-blues-oriented disco singer. It gave me more of an identity. I feel that the pop charts are finally opening to urban contemporary sounds like Herbie Hancock and all those people who are making great street records. Detroit has always been hip to it, but finally mid-America is hearing it for the first time. They're letting go of the race barriers. Now a lot of white people are getting into the dance and rhythm-and-blues charts. Michael Jackson killed the world, and I think it's a good sign!''

During this same period, Madonna penned a song that she felt had the ''urban contemporary'' street beat that no one could seem to comprehend was coming from this hot-looking white soul singer. The song was titled ''Everybody,'' and the demo that she recorded with Steve Bray was all that she had to show for the effort that she had put into the band she christened with her nickname, Emmy.

She wasn't interested in becoming a Pat Benatar clone, so Emmy broke up. Says Madonna, ''I finally said, 'Forget it. I can't do this anymore. I'm going to have to start all over.' ''

Madonna and Steve Bray stuck together and became regular habitués at the hip-hop dance clubs in Manhattan. Friday nights they would hang out at The Roxy, a former disco roller rink on West Eighteenth Street that drew a black dance crowd. On other nights they would hang out at Danceteria, a funky four-floor rock club on West Twenty-first Street. It was at Danceteria where a chance meeting changed Madonna's career.

4

A Certain Sacrifice

RIGHT AFTER MADONNA RETURNED from Paris in the summer of 1979, she decided to take control of her career as a musician, a singer, and/or an actress. Whatever happened first, and more successfully, was to be what she was going to go with. At the time, she was doing anything that she could to stay afloat in New York City. She even ended up modeling nude for art classes. According to her, "You got paid ten dollars an hour versus a dollar fifty at Burger King. I kept saying, 'It's for Art!'"

This was not a high point for Madonna at all. She recalls her life in a rehearsal building, "It didn't have a bathtub. I bathed in the sink. I slept curled around amplifiers in a sleeping bag. I wore the same thing every day."

Around this time, an aspiring young filmmaker named Stephen Jon Lewicki decided that he was going to take his super-8 camera, round up a cast, and make an experimental avant-garde movie. The film was to be titled *A Certain Sacrifice*. Recalling his original plot concept, Lewicki laughs. "I started off with the idea of human sacrifice, and worked back to Madonna!"

Lewicki placed casting notices in the two main acting trade newspapers, *Back Stage* and *Show Business*, and awaited the responses. Thinking back to the exact wording of the ad he ran in the trade papers, he says, "I don't remember exactly, but I do remember I was looking for a dark-haired woman, 'dominatrix type.' I think I said it, I don't remember exactly, but I was at least hinting at that if I didn't say exactly dominatrix. Plus, exotic dancers and miscellaneous other characters and a middle-aged man. Madonna sent me a letter and photographs."

What he does remember clearly is the handwritten letter that Madonna wrote to him on lined yellow legal-pad paper. When I interviewed Stephen in February 1985, he brought the letter over to my apartment as well as the photos Madonna originally sent him in reply to the trade-ad casting call. The letter read as follows:

Dear Stephen:

I was born and raised in Detroit, Michigan, where I began my career in petulance and precociousness. By the time I was in the fifth grade, I knew I either wanted to be a nun or a movie star. Nine months in a convent cured me of the first disease. During high school, I became slightly schizophrenic, but I couldn't choose between

"class virgin" or the other kind. Both of them
had their values as far as I could see. When I was
fifteen, I began taking ballet classes regularly,
listening to Baroque music, and slowly but surely
developed a great dislike of my classmates, teach-
ers, and high school in general. There was one
exception, and that was my drama class. For one
hour every day, all the megalomaniacs and ego-
tists would meet to compete for roles and argue
about interpretation. I secretly adored when all
eyes were on me, and I could practice being
charming or sophisticated, so I would be pre-
pared for the outside world. My infinite impa-
tience graduated me from high school one year
early, and I entered the fine arts school at the
University of Michigan, studying music and
participating regularly in most theatrical productions. [She went on to explain her Paris adventure, and then ended with] I came back to New
York. I've been here three weeks now, working
with my band, learning to play the drums, taking
dance classes, and waiting for my twentieth
birthday. . . . Is that all?

—MADONNA CICCONE
  Height: 5′ 4½″
  Weight: 102
  Hair: Brown
  Eyes: Hazel
  Birthdate: August 16, 1959

Enclosed in the letter were three photographs of Madonna. Two of the photos were standard color prints of

a $3'' \times 5''$ size. One photo shows Madonna in a pink striped leotard with her arms raised in a dance motion. One $8'' \times 10''$ black-and-white, full-body shot shows Madonna with short brown hair, but it was the second $3'' \times 5''$ shot that clinched the deal. The color photo was of Madonna sitting on a New York City public transport bus, applying bright red liquid lipstick with her finger. The picture is very sexually suggestive, just by the way her finger teasingly brushes across her lips.

According to Lewicki, ''The picture of her, where she's putting lipstick on on the bus, really grabbed my attention. I took one look at it, and I had seen literally two hundred trashy eight-by-ten so-called 'professional' head shots, and they were all, like, girls from New Jersey trying to be actresses, who, just by looking at the photographs had absolutely no talent—or if they did, it was not apparent!

''I took one look at the picture of Madonna, and then I read the letter, which was a very revealing, very vulnerable kind of letter, and it was the most personable communication that I got from anybody. She gave me her life story in two pages, handwritten, which is pretty amazing! It just seemed like it was a fated kind of thing. She must have been pretty curious to have written a two-page letter that was that revealing.

''So I called her up, and we got together down at Washington Square Park.''

Continues Lewicki, ''Madonna thinks that everybody's impressed with her. Her impression of the world is: 'The world is impressed with me!' And that's how she views things. On one hand, I was impressed with her. I was looking for something very specific, and she was exactly what I was looking for—this kind of nasty, sexually charged, at the same time vulnerable female. On one hand, it was kind of a fantasy that I had at the time. At the same time I immediately got the impression from Madonna that there was a lot more trouble to that than meets the eye."

"Did you decide to cast her immediately?" I ask Stephen.

"There was no question!" he exclaims.

The plot of *A Certain Sacrifice* deals with the main character, Dashiel (Jeremy Pattnosh), a young kid from the suburbs who comes from a hostile family life and can't seem to fit in at the preppy Ivy League college where he is enrolled. So he hitchhikes to New York City, where he immediately meets and falls for Rhonda (Madonna Ciccone). When we first see Madonna, she is dancing in a fountain in Washington Square Park, giving us her "Martha Graham does a wet T-shirt competition" interpretative dance. She is wearing a red T-shirt, has stringy, medium-length hair, and she and Jeremy end the scene making out in the water.

In the next scene Dashiel goes into a seedy diner, and a bizarre middle-aged man who won't shut up sits down next to him. The man introduces himself as Raymond Hall. The man is clearly a crazed bigot and the villain of the film. The essence of their conversation ends with Raymond's question "Where can I get laid?" The scene seems to go on forever! By the end of the confrontation, the film's viewers already want Raymond Hall dead!

Cut to an outrageous theater rehearsal/sex orgy in which a man, a drag queen, and a woman aggressively seduce an innocent young girl. In the scene, which is the sixty-minute film's most controversial, we find twenty-year-old Madonna playing the sex object in an erotic episode where she bares her breasts and has multiple orgasms with her proclaimed "family of lovers." The sex in the scene is really implied and in no way can be construed as pornographic—just a lot of groping and flashing.

The next scene features Madonna and Jeremy. In it she explains that she loves him, but she doesn't know how she is going to explain this monogamous infatuation to her "family of lovers."

"They idolize me," she confesses. "I can't get out of the group-sex scene." Madonna's best line in the whole film comes when she asks, "Do you think for once that any lover of mine could be tame? It's not possible!" She adds, explaining about her "lovers," "They're like irritated hornets, and they want to sting!" It's a remarkably subtle scene, with Madonna playing a warm, vulnerable role with a great degree of honesty.

In the film, oddly, both Jeremy and the woman who plays his landlady wear crucifixes. Madonna for once does not!

It seems that Raymond Hall has been spreading rumors about Dashiel, and Dashiel ends up thrown out of his apartment and is reduced to sleeping on a park bench. Cut to the same scuzzy local diner as before. We see Raymond arguing with the girl behind the counter. In the same diner, Madonna and Jeremy (Dashiel) are kissing at the table in the front window. Madonna goes into the dingy bathroom to fix her lipstick and ends up raped by Raymond Hall. Madonna emerges from the bathroom with her face smeared with blood, and she is crying and screaming hysterically. "He will pay!" Dashiel vows.

Madonna, Dashiel, and the "family of lovers" hijack a black Cadillac stretch limousine and, looking for vengeance, scour the city for Raymond Hall. "He's scummier than any scum!" ad-libs Madonna as they corner Raymond in front of a sleazy porno-theater doorway. The five vengeance seekers drag Hall into the limo and proceed to prepare for a vigilante-style human sacrifice under the Brooklyn Bridge. The sacrifice scene is—are you ready for this?—a musical number entitled "Raymond Hall Must Die Today!" After the murderous rock number, Rhonda (Madonna) and Dashiel (Jeremy) live happily ever after. Bizarre, but fun!

Says filmmaker Lewicki of Madonna's experimental-movie debut, "She had energy, she had charisma. She's got these sparkling eyes. At the time she had this dark brunette hair that was very attractive. She was a very appealing, very sexual person. She works well on film, and I knew that instantly. It was just an immediate thing.

"Whatever differences I had with Madonna," continues Stephen, "I will always say she was very professional. Madonna loves to have the camera pointed at her. She needs a lot of attention, and that gives her that kind of [star] quality. That's the deepest need that I think she has as a person. That fulfills her. She's probably a very fulfilled person right now, because she has the entire world looking at her. That's her fantasy. She wants to be a movie star. She wants to be a STAR. The medium doesn't really matter to her as much as the fact that people are paying attention to her."

According to Stephen Lewicki, the filming of *A Certain Sacrifice* went from October 1979 to November 1981. The script was written as he went along, and the filming was done in pieces, as he came up with the cash for the film.

To say that this was a low-budget production is an understatement, yet many of the scenes are quite effective. As Stephen explained his budget to me, "The only person I paid was Madonna! I paid her a hundred dollars, and that was when she finally agreed to do the last three scenes that I wanted her to do, which was the rape scene and a couple of other scenes that I wanted her to do. After she agreed to do it, she said, 'Well, I want a hundred dollars.' She needed the hundred dollars to pay her rent; she told me that. She was living with Steve Bray in a loft on Thirty-sixth Street or something like that at the time. She had broken up with Dan Gilroy, and she needed the money.

"I called her up, and I said, 'Madonna, there's this other scene I want to shoot,' and she'd say, 'Oh, Stephen, isn't this done yet?!' She would give me all this, and I would placate her on the phone for ten minutes, and then she'd finally agree to do it. Then when she did it, she was very, very good."

Lewicki observes, "She was totally undeveloped, and I was totally undeveloped, so we kind of had this sort of 'pissy' attitude toward each other. We'd kind of insult each other a little bit along the way, but I really don't know how Madonna feels about me at this point. She has no particular need for this movie. If anything, it's sort of a thorn in her behind. I have a theory, and that is that this is a good thing for her because there's a lot of people out there who percieve Madonna as being the creation of Warner Brothers Records, which is not true. But Warner Brothers, from what I gather, they have this feeling that they created this thing. And they think, all right, Madonna had something when she came to us, but of course we polished her up and made her what she is. But I think, for Madonna, for her fans who really like Madonna, this movie is an important thing, because it shows what Madonna was before she had any contact with record companies or makeup people or anything that had to do with being professional. Aside from the people in Paris, who really kind of set her off in the wrong direction, that was the closest that she ever got to any professional contact.''

When I ask Stephen if there were any ego battles during the filming, he explains, ''There was no 'attitude' around the set. We just did this thing: got out the super-8 camera and filmed it, and the batteries would go, and I wouldn't have any extra batteries, and Madonna would shout, 'Goddamn it, Stephen, can't you keep extra batteries?' ''

Another interesting point that Stephen brought up was the fact that Angie Smit, one of the other members of Madonna's early musical group Breakfast Club, was also in *A Certain Sacrifice*. Said Lewicki, ''Angie came with Madonna. She played one of the sex slaves. Madonna and Angie had a really intense relationship, almost like sisters, mother-daughter-lover or something. It was a very complicated relationship, very tight. They would walk together and chew gum at the same time! There was just a real closeness, intensity about the relationship, and I don't know anything about what was going on. They were doing the Breakfast Club thing while I was doing this movie. As a matter of fact, I went to see her a couple of times at different venues. That's when she was playing with Angie and Dan Gilroy and his brother Ed.''

According to Lewicki, shortly after the film was completed, Madonna and Angie had a falling out. Apparently Angie got involved with a real druggy set of people, and Madonna wasn't interested in having anything to do with it or Angie. Stephen explains, ''I remember Angie telling me that Madonna had just become a real bitch—just too much of an egotist—but there are two sides to that story. I met Angie's boyfriend, and he was a real ass, so I can see Madonna's side of it.''

Stephen Lewicki is trying to get people interested in broadcasting, excerpting, or distributing *A Certain Sacrifice* based on its being Madonna's film debut. He is quite realistic about it, however, and doesn't expect it to become a major feature film. As though Madonna needs another Marilyn Monroe parallel, *A Certain Sacrifice* may just end up being to Madonna what Marilyn's now-famous nude calendar shot was to her!

A Certain Sacrifice is a real collector's item to view. It is an important documentary in Madonna's career, because it clearly illustrates a close look at Madonna Ciccone, circa 1979—ready to explore any avenue available in her quest for stardom.

5

"Everybody"

IT WAS DURING ONE OF HER late-night dance excursions at the rock club Danceteria that the tide changed in Madonna's career. During the winter of 1981–82, Madonna was frequenting the dance floor at the club and caught the eye of the disk jockey, Mark Kamins. The meeting was fated.

According to Kamins, "She was one of my dancers, you could say. There was a crowd out there that came every Saturday night to dance—but she was special." Looking back on those nights, Kamins adds, "Madonna was special—young and a little bit naive. She had her own style, always with a little belly button showing, the net top, and the stockings. But she always knew what she wanted to do. She had a tremendous desire to perform for people. When she'd start dancing, there'd be twenty people getting up and dancing with her."

Madonna with a wink, admits, "I was flirting with him!"

As the story goes, Madonna just happened to have with her a copy of a four-track demo that she and Steve Bray had been working on. After talking and flirting with Kamins for a while, she convinced him to put her demo on at the club. It was a rough mix of the song she had written, titled "Everybody." The reaction was phenomenal, and Kamins knew that he had a dance-floor hit pouring out of the speakers of Danceteria.

He made a pact with Madonna right then and there, and the two of them went into the studio and produced a "new and improved" version of "Everybody," with the slick quality that would allow it to be submitted to a record label.

The man to whom Kamins took Madonna and her new recording of "Everybody" was Seymour Stein, president of Sire Records, which is a division of Warner Brothers Records. Stein just happened to be in a New York hospital at the time, but that didn't dissuade any of the interested parties. Recalls Stein, "I was in the hospital when I heard about Madonna. From what I'd heard, I wanted to meet her immediately. So Mark Kamins brought her in, and I signed the contract there, right in the hospital. But I shaved, I combed my hair, I got a new dressing gown. From what I'd heard, I was excited to meet Madonna! And there was something that set her apart immediately. She was outgoing, strong, dynamic—self-assured."

The contract started out as a "singles" deal to see how Madonna would be received, with an option for an album if the records sold well. Released in April 1982 "Everybody," was the first of the three disco twelve-inch singles to be released (followed by "Burning Up" and "Physical Attraction"), and it ended up number three on the American dance charts. The original twelve-inch single of "Everybody" had a photo-montage picture sleeve that did not have Madonna's picture on it, so everyone who heard it assumed that she was black, due to her soulful delivery on the vocal.

Although it was Mark Kamins who produced the ultimate version of "Everybody" for Sire Records, Steve Bray was ecstatic because Madonna had promised him that he would produce the album. Well, everybody was in for a surprise, because when it came time to decide on a producer for the follow-up to "Everybody," Madonna dumped both Kamins and Bray, and signed Reggie Lucas instead.

Recalls Madonna, "I was really scared. I thought I had been given a golden egg. In my mind I thought, 'Okay, Mark can produce the album and Steve can play the instruments.' " Steve had it in his mind that he wanted to produce the album too. Continues Madonna, "It was really awful, but I just didn't trust him enough. Steve didn't believe in the ethics of the situation."

Steve Bray ended up remaining friends with Madonna in spite of his hurt feelings, but he adds, "The relationship's too old to have something like that stand in its way. Exploited? People say that, but that's resentment of someone who's got the drive. It seems like you're leaving people behind or you're stepping on them, and the fact is that you're moving and they're not. She doesn't try to be that polite. She doesn't care if she ruffles someone's feathers."

On a similar count, after the success of "Everybody," Madonna announced that she wanted Reggie Lucas to produce the rest of the album. Lucas felt that if it was a huge success, he would get to do Madonna's follow-up album as well. After the album *Madonna* became such a huge success, which it of course did, Madonna turned her back on Lucas as well and hired Nile Rodgers. Reggie Lucas recalls what he thought after he heard "Everybody": "I wanted to push her in a pop direction. She was a little more oriented toward the disco thing, but I thought she had appeal to a general market. It's funny about that thing with Kamins. The same thing that happened to him pretty much happened to me on her second record, when they had Nile Rodgers."

In the middle of January 1985, I interviewed Mark Kamins about the whole Madonna story and his involvement in it. He was quite complimentary about her and her talents, and diplomatically denied that there was any animosity between the two of them. As a producer, his involvement in her career has clearly put him on the map, and he hopes that they will one day work together again. Here's what Kamins told me about Madonna.

BEGO: You met Madonna at Danceteria?
KAMINS: Yeah, she was one of the regulars who
                   came to the club quite often.
BEGO: As I understand it, she showed up one
                   night with an audition tape of hers.
KAMINS: It was just a tape she was working on.
                   That was "Everybody," and she brought
                   it up to the booth and I listened to it,
                   played it, and got a great reaction.

BEGO: Who had produced that original version
           of it?

KAMINS: She did.

BEGO: Was that with the band she was working
           with?

KAMINS: Steve Bray.

BEGO: And what was your reaction to it?

KAMINS: It was a great little record. And then I
           wanted to make a recording of it. I
           brought it to Sire Records, to Seymour
           Stein, and he liked it and we went in the
           studio. That's how it all started.

BEGO: At that time had she done the video of
           "Everybody," and did you work on it?

KAMINS: No, Ed Steinberg did that. They shot it at
           the Garage [Paradise Garage, a disco in
           lower Manhattan].

BEGO: So she basically had just a rough tape?

KAMINS: A four-track demo.

BEGO: What was it that you thought at the time?
           Was it the song or Madonna that you
           liked?

KAMINS: It was a great song and she had a great
           voice. And plus, I knew she wasn't signed
           [to a record contract]. And she had that
           quality about herself, so there was an aura
           that was surrounding her even at that stage.

BEGO: My understanding of the story is that she
           said if you helped her get a record deal,
           you would be producing the album.

KAMINS: That was always understood, but the
           record company wanted to use a producer
           with more experience than myself.

BEGO: How did you get the deal producing
            "Everybody"?

KAMINS: Well, Seymour believed in me. So he
            said, "Okay, give it a shot."
            "Everybody" was actually a B side.
            There was an A side called "Ain't No Big
            Deal." "Everybody" was supposed to
            be the B side, but it came out so great!

BEGO: Madonna's recording of "Ain't No Big
            Deal" is on the B-side compilation album
            Revenge of the Killer B's, Volume 2.

KAMINS: Yeah, even Reggie did a version of it.
            They used Reggie's version of it. I have a
            version of that that's never ever been
            released.

BEGO: So, did you just produce the two songs?

KAMINS: Yes, there's that one version of that song
            that's never been released.

BEGO: So, Sire Records released a twelve-inch
            of "Everybody" as her first release?

KAMINS: Twelve-inch, and I did a nine-minute dub
            mix for the B side, on "Everybody."
            Madonna wrote both of them. You really
            have to be the songwriter these days,
            because I really believe it's the song. It's
            the major part of the record.

BEGO: So you recorded those two songs and took
            them to Seymour, and what happened?

KAMINS: Well, they put it out. They put
            "Everybody" out—the first single. It
            went to number three on the dance charts.
            It was about one hundred two on the pop
            charts. And they went and did a second

single. That's when they picked a new producer. Which, I suppose, looking back, seemes like a wise decision when you see how her career has gone. All the right moves were made. So I ain't got no complaints.

BEGO: It's just amazing. When they threw out "Ain't No Big Deal" and kept "Everybody" and brought in a new producer, did you still have a piece of the album profits?

KAMINS: Yeah. Just because I had signed her to Sire Records, there's a royalty involved.

BEGO: What do you think of the musical direction she's taken now with Nile on the *Like A Virgin* album?

KAMINS: I like the record. It's a little more "poppy" than I expected it to be. But it's a great record. It doesn't have the variety that the first album did. All the songs have the same kind of sound. It's a good record. I think it has a few hits on it. "Material Girl," that's going to be a big record.

BEGO: Are you still in contact with Madonna?

KAMINS: Oh, yeah. I speak to her. I'm producing a girl for Island Records, and Madonna wrote a song for me. Her name's Shane. Her first single will be out in a couple of weeks. The song that Madonna wrote will be her second single. She's wild. It's called "Call Me, Mr. Telephone."

BEGO: Were you present on the shoot for the video of "Everybody"?

KAMINS: No, I was in the studio that day. Right
            after ''Everybody'' came out, I started
            getting a lot of work mixing, producing,
            so my career's kind of taken off.

BEGO: The ''Everybody'' video is quite rare and
            its basically a performance tape, as I
            recall.

KAMINS: I haven't seen it in a long time. It's
            probably a collector's item now. There
            weren't any video shows when that came
            out in July of 1982. So, is she going to be
            a film star [referring to *Desperately
            Seeking Susan*]?

BEGO: I think so. I was on the set a couple of
            days and it looks real good. When I first
            came in, you said something about
            Madonna's star quality. Could you define
            that a little more, circa 1982?

KAMINS: Just that she definitely had her own sense
            of style, of fashion, you know. No one's
            ever told her how to dress. She has a
            natural beauty, and she has a magic.
            She's definitely a survivor, and definitely
            a winner. She knows what she wants to
            do, and if you don't know what you want,
            you ain't going to get it. You have to have
            a goal, you have to know what you want.
            There are many different ways to get it,
            different avenues. I think she's made the
            right decisions—obviously!

BEGO: Do you foresee yourself working with
            Madonna again in the future?

KAMINS: Hopefully. When I'm one of the top

BEGO: producers, it'll all come back. You know—what goes around comes around. So there's no animosity because of what happened with her first album?

KAMINS: No, none at all.

Mae West used to say, "It's not the men in your life, it's the life in your men." Madonna's early career encompassed three main men who helped her get her act in action and get "Everybody" released and on the charts. One of the underlying factors about the men who helped her get started is that although she turned her back on them when she had utilized them, they have all remained charmed by her and just shrug their shoulders to her cold-shoulder routine. Madonna is quite up front about her tactics, as she admits, "I think most people who meet me know that that's the kind of person I am. It comes down to doing what you have to do for your career. I think most people who are attracted to me understand that, and they just have to take that under consideration." As Tina Turner would say, "What's love got to do with it?"

Dan Gilroy, the man who taught her about the music business says, "I think that a lot of people do feel exploited by her. But then again, everyone's got so many expectations about a relationship with her. She's very intense immediately with somebody, very friendly. Perhaps people feel, 'This is what our relationship is about,' and then if there is any cooling of that, it's taken to be a rejection."

Mark Kamins remains quite complimentary, even though he didn't get the promised production deal on the *Madonna* album. "She's a star, and you get where you have to go. She's got a good heart—deep, deep down there,'' he says, obviously still in awe of her star stature.

Steve Bray, who is now her songwriting partner, best sums up Madonna by explaining, ''She's extraordinarily talented, and a friend. But, with her, being polite and ladylike gets left behind.''

It was right after the release of the twelve-inch disco single ''Everybody'' that Madonna met the next important man in her life—romantically and professionally. When she first met him, he was just another New York City discotheque disk jockey for whom she wanted to play her record, but he has turned out to be one of the hottest record producers around. His name is John ''Jellybean'' Benitez.

6

Shaping the Madonna Mystique

"SOMETIMES I HAVE LITTLE pep talks with myself, and I'll say, 'If you don't believe that you're a star and that you're special, no one else is going to!' "—Madonna

Apparently Madonna's little pep talks worked from the very beginning—and everyone believed it. One of the first believers was Jellybean, who at the time, in the fall of 1982, was best known as the star disk jockey at the Manhattan dance club The Fun House. Madonna and Jellybean ended up dating for the next two years.

When I interviewed John "Jellybean" Benitez in November 1984, he recalled their initial meeting. "We met in my DJ booth at The Fun House. Bobby Shaw, who was the dance-promotion person for Warner Brothers, brought her by. I mean, most record companies from the New York market would bring by artists to Jellybean. And when I met Madonna, I was attracted to her right away. We just sort of hit it off—sort of played games with each other. I thought she was just being friendly with me because she wanted her record ["Everybody"] played. And she thought she didn't want to be nice to me because everybody was always nice to me to play their records. So we were just playing little cat-and-mouse games. So that's what happened, and we started going out and the rest is history."

Well, for the pair, the history was just beginning. After their first frosty meeting in the clown's-head-shaped DJ booth at The Fun House, they ran into each other at a concert at The Ritz (a rock palace on East Eleventh Street) and became quite friendly. Aside from his notoriety as a late-night dance-floor DJ, Benitez was also getting quite well-known as a record remixer. He takes the original tapes for songs, adds bass and percussion tracks, extends the song, creates breaks, and comes up with dance-floor hits out of moderately danceable songs. Among the first of his masterpieces were twelve-inch disco versions of Irene Cara's "What A Feeling (Theme from *Flashdance*)" and "Say, Say, Say" for Paul McCartney and Michael Jackson.

Jellybean's notable work with Madonna was just beginning, and eventually he produced the hits "Holiday," "Gambler," and "Crazy For You." However, following "Everybody," Jellybean's first Madonna assignments were as a disco remixer. Benitez recounted to me, "When she did the next record, they [Warner Brothers] asked me to come in, and I did a twelve-inch of 'Physical Attraction.' And when her album [*Madonna*] was done, they asked me to do 'Lucky Star' and 'Borderline,' remixing those songs."

It was that same time that Reggie Lucas produced his version of "Ain't No Big Deal" for inclusion on the *Madonna* album, but the record company nixed the song, so they turned to Jellybean. He recalls, "At the last second they needed one more song to get on the album, and I had like a week, and I said, 'Why don't you let me produce it?' They said 'Okay!' "

"Up until then you had only remixed?" I ask.

"Yeah," Benitez remembers. "They needed one more song, and I had this demo, the song 'Holiday,' and I played it for them, and they liked it a lot and gave me a week to produce it. I worked like twenty hours a day to get it done and finish it. 'Lucky Star' was supposed to be the first single, but there was such a strong reaction in the New York City clubs that they went with 'Holiday.' And 'Holiday' was the song that broke her. Then I went into additional production on 'Borderline,' and then that came out, and then 'Lucky Star' came out." History was in the making for Madonna.

One of the first times I met Jellybean was in February 1983. I was working for Mary Wilson of the Supremes, and I was helping her find a recording deal as a solo act. Mary had found a song that she wanted to record called "This Girl's Back In Town," which Paul Jabara wrote. Since both Jellybean and I have the same publicist, David Salidor, he set up a preliminary meeting. I played "This Girl's Back In Town" for him, and he was unimpressed, but he had this other song that he was hot on doing—it was "Holiday." It had a catchy beat, and the lyrics just kept repeating the lyrics "holiday, celebrate" over and over again. I wondered what Mary was going to think of it, so an additional meeting was set up with all four of us present, the first Friday in

March 1983. Jellybean was very excited about the song and put it on Mary's tape player, and we all gave it a listen. Mary had her heart set on "This Girl's Back In Town" and wasn't thrilled with this demo that just kept repeating "holiday, celebrate." In essence, neither Mary nor Jellybean was excited by the other one's songs, so that was that.

It was in May 1983 that Jellybean went into the studio with Madonna for his super rush session. A couple of months later I turned on the radio and what did I hear? You guessed it: "holiday, celebrate!" being sung by Madonna!

In 1985 Mary Wilson went into the recording studio with Holland, Dozier, and Holland, the producing trio who did the original Supremes hits in the 1960s, and was excited by the results. However, needless to say, she admits, "I kick myself every time I hear that damn 'Holiday' come on the radio!"

Mary shouldn't feel too bad about missing out on that song. According to Jellybean, it was the song that no one liked on the initial listening, but he persisted. "I kept playing it for people and they would say, 'Oh, I don't know.' You know, 'It's not a hit.' It would have been Mary Wilson's first major hit. When people didn't like it, I just didn't care because I knew it was going to be a hit. 'Holiday' was an international hit. It was top five in England, Germany, and Australia, which are the biggest markets outside America," he proclaims. In America the song spent over six months on the pop charts and peaked at number sixteen, and was a number-one smash on the dance charts. The song "Holiday" made Madonna a singing star.

became friends. And since I'm a stylist, she became very involved with me, and I helped her a lot. I did the costume for the MTV look, the MTV Awards. And I did style the last album [cover], *Like A Virgin*. And I don't know if you realized, but I kind of got the soft feeling, because I thought it was interesting to have a wedding dress, and we did that. And so, we did the whole thing, from the bouquet, to the veil, to the hair.

MARK: So, have you been involved in some of her videos as well?

MARIPOL: I wasn't involved in the last video ["Like A Virgin"]. I was involved in the "Burning Up" video scenes, like, picking out the jewelry. I wasn't involved in the last video, even though I was supposed to, because I was in Japan, and so they took along a stylist. But Madonna is very faithful to my look, and she wears my jewelry all of the time. I do make special things for her that I don't sell to the public; special items. I think I'm supposed to do the next video with her, and I really like to work with her. She was just here before.

MARK: How did you come up with the use of crosses and crucifixes in your designs?

MARIPOL: Madonna picked up on it. I started to make crosses during the punk movement in 1979, which was my religious belief also. But just because it was fun to wear it on the ears. It was a punk sign of rejecting religion, that way, by saying, "I'm wearing it where I want to." And I always loved religious symbols. If you think about it, jewelry was always oriented toward religion.

MARK: So you are basically bringing it back into fashion with its original purpose in mind?

MARIPOL: Yes, it's because it's kind of a little voodoo protection, whatever sign. With Madonna it's perfect, because of the name she wears, and she really liked it right away. I guess she assimilated herself to that. The trend was set right after that, because everybody started doing it. It cannot piss me off, because they do it by feeling, they do it by trend—they want to be trendy and copy. But I don't care, it doesn't matter.

MARK: Do you feel that you have to constantly change your jewelry designs because people pick up on what you do?

MARIPOL: No, I do change them, but I like to go on, because a trend becomes a trademark. Like the rubber bracelets and the crosses, people know me for doing that, therefore I cannot stop them. It's like Coco Chanel—you can still see her designs fifty years later. Tomorrow if I'm fed up with seeing an item, I definitely feel very strong about that. I set up the trends, therefore I can stop it whenever I want to! I'm more of a trend-setter than a jewelry designer.

MARK: Was your idea for Madonna to wear the crucifixes and the Stars of David together, or was that her concept of wearing diverse religious symbols together?

MARIPOL: Yes, it's a little voodoo. That was her choice to do that, I'm not really responsible. We do collect rosaries together. Whenever I buy them, or I get them, I give [them to] her.

MARK: If you were to describe in a word how you would like people to think of your fashion sense, what would that word be?

MARIPOL: Fun. Fun to begin with, and aesthetic beauty, I think. It's fun and it's cute. It's nice, not heavy to wear, and practical. When you think about the jewelry—you don't pay a lot of money, therefore it can break or you can use it for this or that.

MARK: In other words, it's living art. You don't have to protect it.

MARIPOL: You don't have to protect it. You can just break it or take your shower with it. We are living in a fast world, and therefore I don't think there is any more room for too much diamonds around. I don't really believe in it. My trademark

> is also because it's a bourgeois thing to
> do costume jewelry—opposite to real
> jewelry. It's very interesting because
> you can buy a lot of them and never
> spend what you would spend if you just
> buy diamonds.

On a fashion note: just in case you want to check into the prices of Maripol's jewelry designs, or if you're just dying for one of those high-fashion crucifixes like the ones Madonna wears, here's the vital info: Maripolitan, 59–65 Bleecker Street, New York, N.Y. 10012. Phone: (212) 475-2277. If you are interested in the black rubber bracelets that everyone is wearing in varying multitudes à la Madonna, you can phone Canal Rubber in New York City at (212) 226-7339. Now you too can dress like a trendy "Lucky Star"!

The *Madonna* Album

Madonna's debut album, aptly titled *Madonna* (Sire Records 1-23867), was released in July 1983 and began its slow ascent up the American record charts. It took a total of fifty-eight weeks to make the climb, reaching the top ten of *Billboard* magazine the week of October 6, 1984. It made the same vault into the top ten in *Cash Box* the week of October 20, 1984, after fifty-six weeks on their charts.

As a recording artist, Madonna began as a disco singer, and at the start of her career, that's where she made the most initial chart impact. Based on her sales figures and chart performance, in the year-end issue of *Billboard* (December 24, 1983), Madonna made the following charts for overall 1983:

Top Dance/Disco Singles/Albums
1. "Billie Jean"/"Beat It"—Michael Jackson
2. "Let's Dance"—David Bowie
3. "Holiday"/"Lucky Star"—Madonna

Top Dance/Disco Artists
1. Michael Jackson
2. Madonna

Already she was in some pretty heady company, competing for the spotlight with Michael Jackson and David Bowie!

The year 1984 was to become the year that Madonna crossed over to the pop and black charts—and she did it in a big way. In the December 22, 1984, issue of *Billboard*, the year-end issue tallied Madonna in the following positions and categories:

Top Pop Albums—*Madonna*, #17
Top Pop Singles Artists—Madonna, #12
Top Pop Album Artists—Madonna, #26
Top Pop Singles by Madonna
       —#35, "Borderline"
       —#66, "Lucky Star"
       —#79, "Holiday"

Outrageously enough, Madonna was the highest rated
nonblack artist on the black charts. The only other
white singer on the black charts was Teena Marie.

Top Black Albums—*Madonna*, #15
Top Black Album Artists—Madonna, #18
Top Black Artists/Combined LPs & Singles
  —Madonna, #39

Competing with the other pop girls who just want to
have fun, Madonna placed herself on two charts at
number three:

Top Pop Album Artists—Female
1. Cyndi Lauper
2. Linda Ronstadt
3. Madonna

Top Pop Singles Artists—Female
1. Cyndi Lauper
2. Tina Turner
3. Madonna

Madonna's first album, and the singles that it bore,
kept her active on the charts for two and a half years!
The *Like A Virgin* album, which was recorded in the
spring of 1984, had to have its release held back because the *Madonna* album was such a smash.

Madonna's initial disco success blossomed into air
play on black and urban-contemporary radio stations.

Because her picture never appeared on the first twelve-inch singles, no one really knew, or for that matter cared, if Madonna was black or white. All that DJs knew was that she sounded soulful. That's how Madonna has always sung. "It was the music that had guts when I was growing up," Madonna proclaims of her Motown roots.

When the album came out, everyone could see another Madonna: the New Wave fashion plate. The black-and-white photos that appear on the *Madonna* album were taken by Gary Heery. Maripol was the stylist, and Carin Goldberg was the art director who put the package together. This was the first solid glimpse at seductive Madonna with her creamy-complected alabaster skin, unruly bleached blonde tresses, sexy pout, and that distinctive little beauty mark floating above the right side of her painted lips. Staring out from the cover of the album, Madonna gives a self-confident yet vulnerable look at the camera. With her raised arms covered in black rubber bracelets and chains, Madonna's mysterious come-on look gave instant birth to the tag "the Marilyn Monroe of the 1980s." Thanks to Madonna—and Maripol's jewelry effects—a star, and a look, was born. On the inside sleeve of the album is a thighs-up shot of Madonna with her arms raised and behind her head, her hair tied in a rag, and her famous navel exposed for all to see.

"Lucky Star" begins side one of the album and sets the pace of the record. Written by Madonna and produced by Reggie Lucas, "Lucky Star" begins with the soaring sounds of harplike synthesizer notes suggesting twinkling stars. Seconds into the synthesizer cascade, a slapping bass beat punctuates the track with a persistent thumping. By the time Madonna and her background girls chime in, the song sounds like a streamlined Motown girl-group classic. The medium-paced smash peaked at number four on the *Billboard* pop chart the week of October 20, 1984.

Next on the album is a song that Reggie Lucas wrote and produced, titled "Borderline." It hit *Billboard's* pop top ten the week of June 16, 1984, and really established Madonna as a pop singles artist. The song again begins with a delicate sound, this time a reverie of chimes that sweeps in to a melodic synthesizer keyboard. On her vocal, Madonna pleads to her lover that she is on the "borderline" of insanity over unrequited love.

The album's next cut, the fast-paced Madonna composition "Burning Up," represents the first song that Reggie Lucas produced for her, when she was still on her singles deal with Sire Records. This is Madonna's peppy, danceable rock number. It is one of the most exciting cuts on the album. With its breathy and suggestive panting and wailing guitars, it represents Madonna's most fiery vocal performance on the album, complete with multitrack vocals from Ms. Ciccone.

Side one ends with "I Know It," another Madonna composition, with Reggie Lucas producing. The song has a steady beat and a crisp sound, and shows off Madonna singing in a bratty "get lost" mood. "I Know It" establishes her famous "love 'em and leave 'em" stance on romance in this poppish and bubbly production.

Side two of *Madonna* opens with the famous song that John "Jellybean" Benitez couldn't get anyone to record: "Holiday." Jellybean's debut as a record producer is a quick-paced multilevel party anthem carried to frothy success with Fred Zarr's bouncy synthesizer, acoustic piano, and fender rhodes keyboard interplays. In the background, Madonna, Tina B., and Norma Jean keep repeating the chorus of "holiday, celebrate," while Madonna gets the whole world to rally and party with her lighthearted lead vocal. The song (written by Curtis Hudson and Lisa Stevens) really succeeds because of Madonna's enticingly fun mood that comes across in the recording.

"Think Of Me," a song that Madonna wrote and Reggie Lucas produced, follows effervescent "Holiday." The pace slows down a bit on "Think of Me," which is a pleasant, medium-paced number whose beat is almost identical to "Holiday's." Bobby Malach's tenor saxophone solo gives the cut a jazzy midsong bridge. Again the production is crisp and clean, and Madonna's vocal is clear as a bell throughout.

Reggie Lucas' production on his composition "Physical Attraction" again has the same synthetic drum pace as the two preceding cuts. This is Madonna's sirenlike come-on song, which features her in a breathy spoken monologue midsong. The cut crackles with sex, to a bump-and-grind pace.

Side two ends with Madonna's first recording, "Everybody." Written by Madonna and produced by Mark Kamins, "Everybody" has a snappy beat and percolating percussion effects, to buoy up Madonna's effortless vocal, which echoes effectively in the background. Again she uses a breathy sex-kitten approach in a spoken passage.

All in all, Madonna's debut album is a progressive dance record, filled with eight medium-paced to fast-paced cuts by three producers, showing off some of the many moods of this newly shining "lucky star." The album has remained a steadily selling hit for two years now, having sold well over two million copies in America alone, thus becoming a certified double-platinum smash. *Madonna* is one of the biggest selling debut albums of the 1980s, and has established one of the decade's sexiest and hottest multimedia stars.

7

Madonna: Our Lady of Rock Video

UNDENIABLY, THE MADONNA sensation has a lot to do with the images she has created in the music-video presentations of her songs. The colorful New Wave babe-in-the-middle-of-the-street in ''Burning Up,'' the bratty street-girl-turned-model in ''Borderline,'' the punk ballet dancer in ''Lucky Star,'' the dewy bride in Venice in ''Like A Virgin,'' and the gold digger in ''Material Girl'' are all musical visions of Madonna that have been vividly brought to life via music video.

Madonna was a video star before she was a movie star, and in many ways she probably is a movie star *because* she was a video star first! Susan Seidelman cast Madonna in *Desperately Seeking Susan* because she had seen Madonna's videos and knew how she was able to successfully make love to the movie camera. Madonna has a face that was meant to be photographed and a myriad of attitudes that perfectly translate to film.

From the very beginning, Madonna picked up on the importance of music videos in the 1980s, and had one of the earliest videos with her debut tune ''Everybody.'' The ''Everybody'' video appears occasionally on television but is more often seen in video bars and clubs. As of this writing, it is not commercially available, and it is not up to the high production values of her later video performances. In ''Everybody'' Madonna and a group of her dancer friends are shown on the stage of the lower Manhattan dance club Paradise Garage. The action all centers around different camera angles of Madonna on stage singing the song. It was basically shot to promote her before she became an album artist.

''Burning Up''

Directed by Steve Baron, with camerawork by King Baggot, this video was very responsible for cementing the Madonna look in the eyes of the world. She is wearing lots of chains and those little black rubber bracelets. Maripol was the stylist on this shooting, so Madonna is swathed in loads of the designer's distinctive jewelry.

The video opens with a series of colorful close-up images: Madonna's eye, a bouquet of daisies, Madonna's red lips, an orange goldfish, Madonna's throat, and finally Madonna dancing about like a whirling dervish. Throughout are interspersed scenes of Madonna in a short white dress, sitting in the middle of a street in the middle of the night. Next, she rolls around in the street while singing the song. Close-ups of Madonna's face are intercut with the action.

One of the most impressive visual aspects is that the color is so dramatic. Madonna's skin is a warm peach color, her lips are bright cherry-red, and her hair has a yellow glow. The video is a showcase for Madonna's dancer/model talents.

At the end of the video, when it appears that Madonna is going to be hit by a car driven by a handsome young man, the film cuts to Madonna driving away, and the guy is nowhere in sight. That incorrigible Madonna—she ditched the guy and kept the car! Bravo!

"Borderline"

This is the first video that Madonna did with director Mary Lambert, who has done some of her most impressive work with Madonna. This is also Madonna's first video with a plot line.

In the story line, we see Madonna dancing in the street with a bunch of kids, looking outrageous in her layers of mismatched clothes and with strips of cloth tied in her hair. A photographer, who has noticed Madonna dancing, introduces himself and gives her his business card. Her boyfriend is clearly not thrilled at the idea of Madonna modeling for the photographer. Naturally, she calls the photographer, and black-and-white photographic sessions alternate with full-color action shots.

We see footage of Madonna and her boyfriend kissing on a rooftop at sunset, then we see Madonna modeling for the successful photographer. She is torn between the two men and the two different life-styles. Does she want the sexy but poor street kid, or the rich and exciting photographer? The boyfriend finds out about the affair when he sees Madonna's face on the cover of a fashion magazine.

One of the best bits of action shows a frustrated Madonna holding on to a street sign and kicking the signpost with her high-heeled shoe, with a bratty scowl on her face. At the conclusion of the video, she ends up going back with her boyfriend. She obviously hasn't become a "material girl" yet!

Director Mary Lambert shows off Madonna very impressively, both in terms of look and character motivation. According to Lambert, she is very conscious of the course of action and the image of the star. She explains, "I try to go for the emotion in the situation and make the image reflect that emotion. You have to avoid clichés to be erotic. It's a cliché that a woman in leather is erotic. It's only erotic if you've evoked an emotion with those images."

"Lucky Star"

This video was directed by Arthur Pierson and filmed by Wayne Isham, and the art director was none other than Madonna. The video of "Lucky Star" is a crisply stark, highly effective dance video. With an all-white no-seams background, Madonna and two other dancers—a guy and a girl—dressed totally in black, perform a frenetic rock ballet to the song "Lucky Star."

Madonna also rolls around on the floor a bit and shows off her belly button. Five-pointed star earrings and crucifixes dangle from her ears, and black rags are tied in her hair. The only true color is the red of Madonna's lips. The starkness of the black outfits against the white backdrop puts the focus on Madonna and the dancers' movements. The exotic dance motions become the focus of the video, and Madonna gets to show off her interpretive dance training. "Lucky Star" is a very stylish video, with some great editing and exciting camera angles.

"Like A Virgin"

This was also directed by Mary Lambert, with a new cinematographer: Peter Sinclair. This video was filmed on location in Venice and intersperses scenes of Madonna in a sexy green outfit, dancing on a gondola whisking along the canals, and then as a virginal bride. According to Madonna, "We just felt that Venice symbolized so many things, like virginity. And I'm Madonna, and I'm Italian. We wanted me to be the modern-day very worldly wise girl that I am. But then we wanted to go back in time and use, like, an ancient virgin. Me, back and forth. It starts off in New York in a boat. And I get off the boat and when I get off it changes to Venice. I keep going back and forth.

"I'm chasing this man," she continues, "who's in a carnival mask. I'm chasing him through Venice. It keeps going back from the way I look right now, to me in a very old, white lace dress. Anyway, I see this man in a lion's mask for carnival, and I keep following him.

I'll go into an alleyway or something, then I'll trans-
form into an ancient character in a gown with a real
lion. We used a real lion in the video, and it was one of
the most dangerous experiences I've ever had. It had
teeth and everything! The lion tamer said it wouldn't
bite me—or at least it hadn't bitten anyone yet.

"We filmed in these ancient ruins in Venice
with pillars and marble buildings. There was water all
around us; we were working on this piece of land that
jutted out into the Grand Canal. So I'm leaning up
against this pillar with this white guaze all over my
face like a veil, and I've got this long white dress on.
The lion tamer is over there behind the cameraman,
and he's coaxing the lion so he'll walk over on my
right side. Then I'm supposed to lift the veil and we're
supposed to look at each other—like it's an animal-but-
man that I'm attracted to. We were supposed to look at
each other, then he would keep walking toward the
lion tamer.

"Well," says Madonna, "the lion didn't do anything he was supposed to do. I kept waiting for the lion
to come up on my right side, trying to pretend I was relaxed and not nervous. Then all of a sudden I felt this
nudge up against my left-hand side. I looked down and
the lion is like RIGHT THERE with his head in my
crotch! I was really frightened because I thought he
was going to take a bite out of me. He wasn't supposed
to get that close.

"So I lifted up my veil and had a stare-down with a
lion! We just glared at each other for three-quarters of
a minute. Then he opened his mouth and let out this
huge roar! I got so frightened that my heart fell in my
shoe!" she exclaims.

Anyway, the setting is classic, the video is classy, and Madonna looks and moves fantastically. At the end Madonna steps off a boat, and suddenly she is back in New York City. She plays to the camera teasingly, and visually toys with your senses.

In December 1984 the video cassette titled *Madonna* was released (Warner Music Video). The four-cut program includes "Burning Up," "Borderline," "Lucky Star," and "Like A Virgin." It became a top-twenty video cassette package, and has sold very well. In February 1985 three new Madonna songs had videos on the air: "Gambler," "Crazy For You," and "Material Girl." The first two videos are from footage shot for the film *Vision Quest*, which Madonna appeared in. "Material Girl," which is covered in Chapter Eleven, was directed by Mary Lambert.

The MTV Music Video Awards

On September 14, 1984, the first annual MTV Awards were given out in a gala presentation broadcast live from Radio City Music Hall in New York City. The show was hosted by Bette Midler and Dan Aykroyd, and the talent included Huey Lewis and the News, Tina Turner, Hall and Oates, Diana Ross, Rod Stewart, Quincy Jones, ZZ Top, and many others.

Madonna was nominated for an award in the category of Best Video by a New Artist for her "Borderline" video. She was competing against Eurythmics' "Sweet Dreams (Are Made Of This)," Cyndi Lauper's "Girls Just Want To Have Fun," Cyndi Lauper's "Time After Time," and Wang Chung's "Dance

Hall Days.'' The award went to Eurythmics, but Madonna ended up with one of the most outrageous five-minute segments of the show!

Right after David Lee Roth accepted the Best Stage Performance video for Van Halen's ''Jump,'' Madonna made her live national television debut. It was one of the most talked-about events of the evening. Dan Aykroyd introduced her by announcing, ''An alumnus of the Alvin Ailey dance group . . . a queen of music and motion . . . and every biker's dream guest rider: Madonna!''

To a sudden excited burst of applause we saw La Madonna herself perched atop a massive larger-than-life three-tiered wedding cake. Next to her stood a mannequin groom, and in her wedding dress and ''Boy Toy'' belt buckle, Madonna was the bride!

Her dress actually consisted of a white lace corset and brassiere. Around her neck were many chains, strings of white pearls, and a couple of her trademark crucifixes. From her left ear dangled a large silver rhinestone-covered star, and from her right earlobe hung a metallic heart and a small crucifix. On her arms were white lace gloves extending up her arm to above the elbow. Her wrists were covered with a host of bracelets. Her skirt was made of translucent white tulle with white hearts on it, and when the lighting was just right, you could clearly see her white garter belt underneath. On her feet were severely pointed white high heels. With a bridal bouquet in her hand, Madonna launched into the public debut of ''Like A Virgin.''

Kicking off her shoes, Madonna began to descend the cake. Tearing off her veil and letting her hair loose, she fell to the floor of the stage, where she rolled around while she sang. With her shoes back on her feet, she stood up and skipped and strutted about the stage, shimmying and shaking her blond-streaked hair.

Then, as if this weren't wild enough, Madonna threw her veil onto the stage floor, straddled it, and gyrated and shook herself like Salome doing the Dance of the Seven Veils to "Like A Virgin." She proceeded to roll around on the floor, finishing the song as her skirt crept up to her waist. The roving cameramen moved right in, and all of America got a great look at Madonna's legs in garters and panties while she writhed on the floor. Well, so much for the "virgin" image.

Returning to the podium, the show's hostess, Bette Midler, cracked, "Now that the burning question of Madonna's virginity has been answered, we are free to go on to even more GAPING questions, such as: How is a video made? We know Madonna's story!" Everyone cracked up with wild laughter.

Madonna was going to make sure that she got noticed that evening, and she sure did. It was a very important night for her because she was officially in the big leagues now!

8

My Interview
with Madonna

On October 8, 1984, I had the opportunity of interviewing Madonna. At the time she was busily working on the film *Desperately Seeking Susan*, and it was Reid Rosefelt, the movie's unit publicist, who set up the meeting. I was interviewing her for a cover story that I was doing for *Modern Screen* magazine.

The interview itself was held in Maripol's loft at Bleecker Street and Broadway in Greenwich Village. On display racks and on wall-display units were many samples of Maripol's jewelry, accessory, and fashion designs. There were of course a multitude of crucifixes and metallic amulets, including designs adapted from many ancient religions, including Egyptology and Christianity, as well as "voodoo" symbols, as Maripol describes them. Also on the wall I spied a metallic chain-link and Mylar-square miniskirt that Kid Creole's Coconuts have worn onstage in shows I had seen.

The loft space looked as if it could be Madonna's jewelry box.

On another wall were magazine-layout pictures of Madonna modeling Maripol's jewelry designs. At another end of the loft Maripol was doing some of her work, and a kitten scurried about the floor as we spoke. When Madonna whisked into the room, it was clear that the star had just arrived.

She was wearing one of her trademark outfits: a Fordham University T-shirt cut off at the midriff to expose her famous navel. A fishnet top was over the T-shirt, offering little covering. She wore knicker-length pants and more jewelry than Tiffany's usually displays in the windows of its Fifth Avenue store—crucifixes, chains, and, of course, a myriad of black rubber bracelets up and down her arms. Around her waist was her controversial belt buckle emblazoned with the words "Boy Toy."

She had just come from a day on the set of the most important film in her short career, and she was anxious to get down to business.

Sitting next to her on a white leather-look vinyl-covered sofa, we briefly discussed Pontiac, Michigan. Changing the subject to her blossoming career, I commented, "Everybody was talking about you on the MTV Awards!"

"That and my underpants!" Madonna exclaimed, rolling her eyes skyward with disdain. "If I ever see those cameramen, I will personally kill them! They unleashed cameramen on the stage; I had no idea they were going to be there. When I rehearsed, there were two cameramen: one was center stage and one was off on the side. When I did the actual show, there were, like, six all over the place. A camera up my dress! A surprise for everyone!''

"How is it to work with Nile Rodgers?" I asked about the producer of her *Like A Virgin* album.

"Great! He's wonderful—real smart and a great musician," explained Madonna, who described the album by commenting, "There are some dance songs on it, but I have two ballads on it, and it's a lot more pop oriented. Nile did it, so everything's got that beat to it. I used a lot of live drums on this album, whereas on the first [*Madonna*], everything was synthesized on drum machines.''

With regard to her role in *Desperately Seeking Susan*, Madonna admitted, "Some scripts you read and you can just see yourself in the role. I can see myself in the role of this really free-spirited, adventurous girl that people follow around. This girl causes trouble—she's exciting and unpredictable, irresponsible, vulnerable.''

She was quick to clarify. "We're not exactly alike. She doesn't have any goal, it seems, except to complicate everyone's life—and I did! I want to be somebody, I have goals and directions. Susan doesn't have an occupation or any skills. She just appears and disappears. That gives her a real enigmatic feeling, a sense of fantasy. I think I have more of a definition about myself.''

With regard to her performing a song in the movie, Madonna explained, "I'll be dancing, and the song we'll be dancing to is a song that I've written. I definitely want to write the title track and maybe one other song. They want someone to do background music, but they want one song that's the theme. I've already written it, and I'm waiting for the moment to give it in.''

Since the plot of *Desperately Seeking Susan* is about a mix-up caused by the personals column of a newspaper, I asked Madonna if she had ever answered one. ''No!'' she snapped. ''Please—I've read them from curiosity.''

Madonna became quite friendly with Rosanna Arquette during the filming of the movie. How do their characters interact in the plot? ''We don't actually meet until the end,'' she explained. ''I find her and she's got all my stuff. She takes over, from about ten minutes into the movie. Everyone thinks she's me because of a jacket of mine she gets from a thrift shop that I've traded for a pair of boots. In it is a key to the locker that holds all my personal worldly belongings. Rosanna gets amnesia after she gets the jacket, so when she wakes up she thinks she's me and goes and gets that stuff and starts dressing like me. She's completely opposite of me. She doesn't smoke cigarettes, but she becomes me. In the end we meet up and we become friends and go away on a vacation together. Rosanna's husband, played by Mark Blum, his name is Gary Glass, I do most of my scenes with him. We connect because he wants to find his wife, and I want to get my stuff back. We become detectives together. Of course, I intimidate him and flirt with him all the time. I move into his house in New Jersey.''

Comparing videos to movies, Madonna explained, ''The only difference is the movie takes longer, and there's dialogue, but in a lot of videos now, people are talking. A video is like a silent movie.''

The conversation segues to the topic of the then

unreleased movie *Vision Quest*. "I just sing in it," explained Madonna. "I sing, I perform in a nightclub that the lead actor and actress come into. They dance a slow dance to a song. I have three songs, but I don't know what they're going to cut out of it." Eventually only "Crazy For You" and "Gambler" made it to the screen.

"Have you always written songs?" I asked.

"I didn't start writing songs till about four or five years ago," she replied.

"You went to U of M?" I queried.

"For a semester," she answered. "I graduated from high school early, I came to New York, I got a scholarship to the Alvin Ailey school, I studied there for the summer. I got a scholarship at U of M and went there for a year and went back to the city and got back into the Ailey school, and that's when I met Pearl Lange and started dancing with her.

"I wanted to be a movie star," exclaimed Madonna in answer to a question about her early ambitions, "but when you grow up in some hick town in Michigan, there's nothing you can do that will make you feel like you're going to be a movie star. I was taking dance, ballet, and jazz classes, and I said, 'I know I can be a dancer.' I was always the lead in every musical and every play in high school. When I graduated I got the thespian award. That's my claim to fame. I was a rebel in school. I didn't really fit in. I hung out with all the misfits and freaks that nobody wanted to hang out with."

Unfortunately, Madonna's father could never see the logic in his daughter's fascination with dance and theater. Madonna continued by explaining, "My father thought it was immodest. He kept telling me how immodest I was. There were talent shows in high school, and I'd perform in them every year, and I'd do one outrageous thing after another. My father would sit and be horrified. One time I put a bikini on and painted my body with fluorescent paint. I painted weird designs all over my body and danced to a Who song with black lights flashing and the lights off. I was in all the plays, and I sang in choir at school. My father, up until about two years ago, was bothering me about going back to the University of Michigan.''

Trying to get this all straight, I asked, "So you came to New York and went back to U of M?''

"I only went back there," replied Madonna, "because there was a ballet teacher who said he would devote all his attention to me, to prepare me so I could go to New York. They had a dance company there, and I took advantage of the situation. Kind of like training for the Olympics!''

The conversation shifted to videos. If she had a preference between videos, records, or movies, which would she choose? The answer, of course, was all of the above. "Right now I'm enjoying making movies more than anything," replied Madonna, "but I miss singing. On my days off, I go work with this guy that I write songs with. I have a deal with Warner Brothers, I have to make several albums, or else! But I give people songs. I write songs for other artists, for other soundtracks. I wrote a song for Jellybean's album [*Sidewalk Talk*]. There's a French singer named Natalie. RCA gave her a worldwide deal. I wrote her next song that they'll release in America. And I'll write the song for this movie [*Desperately Seeking Susan*], and another movie Jellybean's producing the soundtrack for [*Fast Forward*]. I like to keep my hands in everything. My video from the new album [*Like A Virgin*] will be released, and I'll do one for the second single ["Material Girl"]. I have decided on the director: Jean-Paul Goude. He was married to Grace Jones.

"Who directed the 'Like A Virgin' video?" I asked, trying to get every detail I could.

"Mary Lambert," she replied. "She did 'Borderline.' She did Sheila E.'s video ["Glamorous Life"], the Go-Gos' video ["Turn To You"]. If I didn't have video, I don't think all the kids in the Midwest would know about me. It takes the place of touring. Everybody sees them everywhere. That really has a lot to do with the success of my album. If I didn't make great songs and didn't make great videos . . . That's not the only thing that will guarantee your success, but it does allow exploitation. I think that I make consistently good videos."

"Will there be a video album?" I instinctively asked.

"Yes, for Christmas: 'Borderline,' 'Lucky Star,' and the new video, 'Like A Virgin.' I just made the deal a couple of weeks ago." Just as I suspected—she doesn't miss a trick!

She admitted that "Borderline" was her favorite video to date and revealed, "In 'Lucky Star,' none of the dancing was planned—I just did it! Or the black-and-white section in 'Borderline,' and the part in 'Burning Up' when I'm on the road. None of that was planned."

Surprisingly, she proclaimed, "I don't have MTV. I do see videos, I go to Private Eyes [a video club on

West Twenty-first Street]. I haven't seen any good videos lately. I like Sheila E.'s video ["Glamorous Life"].
The last video I went crazy over and wanted to see over
and over again was 'Billie Jean' [Michael Jackson]. The
director [Steve Baron] did my first video, 'Burning
Up.' "

This brought up the subject of a concert tour for Madonna. She proved strongly opinionated on the subject as she explained, "I have to admit I'm not really
thrilled about it, because I'm making a movie, and my
attention's on that. If I go on tour, it means I have to
start auditioning all the musicians, sit for hours and
hours and listen to a bunch of awful musicians, and
then I have to get them to play all my songs right! And
I don't like traveling when I'm working. I love to
travel, but not in a van with a bunch of people!" She's
obviously given this a bit of thought.

"If you did tour," I asked hypothetically, "would
there be a concept to the show?"

"Yes, definitely!" Madonna answered, explaining,
"Up to now, I've sung live to tape and used dancers.
I'd combine dancing with it. I will do a tour eventually. I think I'll go to Japan and Australia in the beginning of next year. It's really bad to tour America in
the winter. It's the worst: you get stuck everywhere!
I'll probably do a major-city American tour in the
spring."

"Do you have a vision of a stage concept?" I delved
for more details.

"Yes, but I'm not telling anyone. It's a long way
off!" she exclaimed.

Has fame posed any changes in her life?

"I can't take the subway," she admitted. "I did up till

a few months ago. Now it's really a pain. I take a cab everywhere, and I hate taking cabs. I ride my bike a lot too. It's really hard when you go to restaurants and everyone stares. I don't want people staring at me. I want to eat! Or standing in line at the grocery store, and people are looking to see what you're buying, or when you're in a clothing store and everyone wants to see what you're buying. I just leave. It turns a lot of things off to me.'' You wanted to be famous! I thought.

What kind of mail does Madonna receive?

"I get a lot of stuffed animals for some reason," she said. "I get a few crucifixes. Mostly I just get letters. I don't have a fan club yet. It has to be worked out with this merchandising deal for posters and stuff. I get fan mail sent to my manager [Freddie DeMann] and my agent and my record company—mostly kids, and equal girls *and* boys. The girls gush more than the boys. They write ten-page letters. They tell me what they wear, from the top of their head to the bottom of their toes. They send me pictures of themselves dressed like me. They tell me that somewhere up in Washington they had a Madonna look-alike contest, and they won. Stuff like that. Really funny! They say they've got new boyfriends now because they dress like me.''

"Does that make you feel like you have a responsibility to maintain your image?" I asked.

"Sure," Madonna replied, "but I also think it's good to change. Not always stay the same. The thing that I feel is different about my image versus someone like Annie Lennox [Eurythmics] or Cyndi Lauper, I don't have a really bizarre image. You don't have to chop your hair off or dye it some absurd color to look like me. Maybe that makes it easier or more accessi-

ble. But I also think that will guarantee me more lon-
gevity. I can make a transition into something else.
Can you imagine Boy George with short hair and tight
leather pants? No one will accept that. You paint yourself into a corner when you do stuff like that.''

What are Madonna's strongest musical influences?
"A lot of Motown. All the AM stations in Detroit,
that's all they played. I heard it all the time. I also listened to 'poppy' records too: the Archies, Gary Puckett and The Union Gap, Bobby Sherman. I wasn't into
the Beatles or heavy metal. I loved the song 'Take A
Letter Maria,' 'Incense and Peppermints.' My older
brothers listened to heavy metal all the time and weird
fusion jazz: Mahavishnu Orchestra. I hated that.''

About her early family life, Madonna explained, "It
was like living in a zoo, kind of. You have to share
everything. I slept in a bed for years—not even a dou-
ble bed—with two sisters. My stepmother had a thing
about buying. She'd go out and buy us all the same
thing—the same ****ing outfits. Then I had to wear
uniforms to school. I was dying for some individual-
ity." Elaborating on her family, Madonna explained
of her siblings, "They're not really performers, but
they're talented in other ways. My brother Christopher
came here to be a dancer. He's in my 'Lucky Star' video—he dances behind me. He danced for a couple of
years in a dance company in Canada, and then he came
to New York. He decided he wanted to do something
more challenging. He writes short stories and wants to
get into directing and writing screenplays. He works as
a production assistant to Limelight Videos. He's
worked on some of my videos. He also does PR work
here for Maripol—she does all my jewelry. He's trying

to find his niche. He's been here [New York City] for about four years now, and my sister just moved here. She's living with me right now. She's a graphic artist.''

What musical instruments does Madonna play? Quite a few, actually. "I used to play everything!" she laughed. "I was a drummer my first job in a band. I did that for about a year and a half. All that time I was learning how to play guitar. When I got my own band and was the lead singer, I played guitar. Then I played keyboards, enough to write on. I stopped playing drums and guitar 'cause I don't want to do that in performance. I just play synthesizer to write on.''

"So, how did you make the transition from dancing to singing?" I asked.

"The question everyone asks," said Madonna. "So long and involved!" she sighed in resignation, and then she launched into the explanation. "I just got tired of dancing, and I knew I could sing, and I wanted to be a total performer. I thought of musical theater, and I started reading trade papers and going to auditions Off Broadway. I saw an ad in the newspaper for this French singing star, Patrick Hernandez. He had this record, 'Born To Be Alive.' " I nodded in acknowledgment, and she continued, "His record company was trying to put together an act to go on this world tour with him, and they wanted girls to sing backup vocal and dance. It was going to be this big gala performance. I thought this would be great—I'd be dancing and singing, *and* traveling around the world. I'd never been out of America! So I went to the auditions, and after they were over, they said they didn't want me for Patrick Hernandez. They wanted to bring me to Paris and make me a star! So I went to Paris, and they *didn't* make me a star.

"They promised me everything," she continued. "They said, 'Come to Paris. We'll give you everything you want. You'll live like a queen. We'll give you a vocal coach, and you'll decide what direction you want to go in!' I did live like a queen, and they did give me anything I wanted. It was the only time I lived comfortably my entire life. This was like four years ago. So I went to Paris, but I missed my friends, and I missed struggling. I was used to really working hard, and they wanted to spoil me, and they wanted me to dress a certain way. So they dragged me to restaurants, and no one would speak English to me. So once again I was playing the part of a rebel; I didn't want to do anything they wanted me to do. I gave my money away to people. I hung out with low lifes. I rode around on motorcycles all the time. I did everything I could to be bad. I kept saying, 'When are you going to do something with me?' And they were too busy with Patrick. Every time I complained, they gave me money. I never signed a contract, so I wasn't obligated to stay there. So I waited to see what would happen, and meanwhile I was starting to write a lot—lyrics and stuff. But I didn't really have an idea of what direction I was going to go in musically. I didn't know how to play an instrument. I asked for a holiday to go back to New York to see my friends—and I didn't come back. I got to New York, and I met some musicians, and I said, 'Teach me how to play!' These two brothers—Dan and Ed Gilroy—they lived in a synagogue in Queens. The rabbi died, and they rented out the place in Flushing Meadows."

She continued, "They had a band, and downstairs they had a little recording studio. They would go to work every day, and I would stay there. I lived like a hermit for a year. I didn't leave Queens. I'd play the drums for four hours. They taught me basic chord progressions on piano. As soon as I learned to play guitar a little bit, songs came out of me. I don't know where they came from! It was like magic. I'd write a song every day. I said, 'Oh, wow! I must be meant to do this!' I stopped taking dance classes. When I was in Paris, I was still studying dance.

"I miss being in really great shape," Madonna explained of her lack of exercise since dropping dance classes. "I work out still. I stretch out, and I ride bikes. Sometimes I run, I do a lot of stuff. But I was dancing eight hours a day. I was in great shape. You can't do that when you're playing music. You sit around all the time in the recording studio, eat Cheese Doodles. It forces you to have bad habits. You stay out late. But making movies is totally different from that. You have to get up early. I can adjust, but I can stay out late on weekends, and it's hard on Monday! The rest of the week is okay."

According to Madonna, the most difficult aspect of moviemaking is "just sitting around and not feeling like you're useful all the time on the set. I read books. I do lots of sit-ups in the trailer. I make phone calls from pay phones. But it doesn't bother me. I'm doing what I want to do. I would like to work the whole time I'm on the set. They get you in in the morning, and you're all made up, and you don't work till after lunch. Or you have one scene really early in the morning, and you don't work again till five, and you're just sitting there.

You can't screw up your makeup or your costume! I'm a hyperactive person. I'm used to dancing eight hours a day, and now I'm sitting around eight hours a day. It's really an adjustment.''

Madonna revealed that afternoon that the type of film role she would next like to tackle would be ''something more emotionally demanding. I'd like to have some crying, screaming scenes!''

''Do you want to write a screenplay?'' I asked, figuring that she was involved in every other aspect of her career.

''I'm doing one with some other people. It'll be a movie loosely based on my life, but not exactly,'' she said, not missing a beat.

I gave her a look like, ''Oh, God—not *Purple Rain, Part II*!''

''It's not going to be a Prince movie, don't worry!'' she snapped back. ''Better: *Red Fire*!'' She laughed. ''It'll incorporate all my talents. I'm going to dance in it, sing in it.''

According to Madonna, her favorite type of films are in the *film noir* category. You know, those moody, dark, mysterious films like Fritz Lang's *M*.

Returning to the subject of *Desperately Seeking Susan*, Madonna described the behavior of her character by announcing, ''I'm making out in every other scene! I don't sing in the movie, but I eat Cheese Doodles a lot. I'm always stuffing my face in this movie— constantly! I spit a lot of it out. In the morning I do not want to eat gumdrops and Cheese Doodles! She's really a pig, you know,'' referring to Susan. ''She eats all the time, always has something in her mouth, whether it's a cigarette, a drink.''

"Have you gained weight?" I asked, referring to her having to eat all those Cheese Doodles.

"No," she answered, "but I get up every morning and swim before I go down to the set."

Has she ever had jobs outside of the entertainment industry?

"What?! Are you kidding? For sure! For a long time, until I got my record deal, I was working at all sorts of stupid jobs. I worked at Dunkin' Donuts, I worked at Burger King, I worked at an Amy's [Greek fast food]. I had a lot of jobs that lasted one day. I always talked back to people, and they'd fire me. I was a coat-check girl at the Russian Tea Room for a long time. I worked at a health club once for a week, and I used to model a lot for an art school: the Art Students' League. I had to take my clothes off!"

Did the nudity pose any problems for her?

"Sometimes," she admitted, "if I was in a bad mood. It's the same as being recognized on the street. Sometimes you're in the mood for everyone to know who you are, and other times you feel really vulnerable and you don't want anyone to look at you. At that time I was dancing too, so I would dance all day and go to these drawing classes at night—just walk in there and strip! It was good practice, actually, for my future husband!" she laughed sarcastically. "You have to remove yourself from everyone looking at you," she rationalized. "It's a job. But I knew that those people were not just looking at me aesthetically."

"Do you have a business sense?" I inquired.

"It's not very good," she admitted, adding, "If someone says, 'You're getting a half-million-dollar advance,' I go, 'Big deal!' I don't care. I'm not interested as long as I have enough money to pay the rent and buy all my rubber bracelets and stuff! I'm not really money oriented. That's probably bad because I should be thinking about making investments, but I don't. I'm not really material oriented. I forget I'm spending more than my credit card has left. I bounce checks all the time. I used to borrow money from people. I'd let some poor sucker take me out to dinner and then I'd go, 'Can I borrow a hundred dollars?' I was always borrowing twenty-five, fifty, one hundred dollars from people.''

Now that's what I call a "material girl"! Speaking of material objects, I asked. "What about a line of Madonna merchandising?"

"Posters and buttons," she confirmed, "a jewelry line. We're trying to do that with Maripol right now."

What does Madonna do with her spare time? According to her, "I like to go out to eat, I like to swim, I like to sweat, have a really good workout. I dance in front of my mirror in my house. I have a big loft with no furniture in it and mirrors on the wall. I listen to the radio, and I listen to my own music and tapes of certain songs I get from my record company, but I don't buy records. I don't have a record player."

"Listening to the radio do you get a sense of what's commercial?" I asked.

"Definitely!" she exclaimed. "It's good to hear what people are buying."

Since leaving Pontiac, Michigan, Madonna has gotten a chance to travel a bit. First with Patrick Hernandez, now with her own career. What places would she like to visit in the future?

"I've been to Morocco," Madonna replied, "and

I'd like to go back there when I'm not working—do more exploring. I'd like to go back to Venice. And I haven't been to Australia or Japan or Indonesian countries, and I'd like to go to all those places. Forget the rest of Europe, though. I'm not interested. I've gone to Europe millions of times in the last few years, doing promotional tours and interviews. I like Italy, actually, but I hate all that European pretension. I'd rather deal with a rude, up-front American.''

I gave her eclectic outfit a visual once-over and then discovered that we both have a passion for England when I asked, "Do you do all your clothes shopping here in the Village?''

"No,'' she snapped. "In England I buy a lot of things. The other person that was dancing with me in 'Lucky Star' [the video], she designs a lot of clothes for me. And I like to go to athletic sportswear shops. I hate SoHo [a trendy art and shopping area in New York City]. I never buy anything in SoHo; it's so unoriginal and boring. See all the people who come down there on the weekend? They're from Connecticut and New Jersey and Long Island. Why should I dress like that? I'd rather have original designs: Jean-Paul Gauthier, Azzedine Alaia, Vivian Westwood, Body Map—a lot of English designers.''

What about the clothes that she wears in *Desperately Seeking Susan*? How much input did she have in the "look" of her character?

"I have a lot of input,'' she confirmed. "I wear a lot of my own. In the beginning, the costumes Santo [Loquasto] had gotten for me were things . . . I never would have dressed that way. They were from vintage shops, like Cyndi Lauper dresses,'' she said, making a face like she is going to be sick at the thought of dressing like Cyndi. "Like lots of layers of antique clothing. I hated it! Stiletto heels and stuff. So now I wear a lot of my own accessories. I have rags tied in my hair, tights in my hair. I wear a pair of men's trousers. I didn't want to wear these fifties dresses: chiffon black dresses. I put together things—like one outfit will be my shirt, their skirt, my socks, their shoes. It's a combination."

Now that she had became a bona fide movie star, was there anyone that Madonna would like to work with on the screen?"

"Director-wise," she pondered out loud, "I'd love to work with [Francis Ford] Coppola, [Martin] Scorsese, Bob Fosse. Actor-wise, I'd like to work with Mel Gibson. He's a great actor, and he's great looking—and he's normal. He doesn't seem like he has any weird . . . He's not like Matt Dillon!" she says with disgust. "Mel Gibson is past that, he's not an arrogant, snot-nosed brat."

Since everyone is singing duets nowadays, can we look forward to one from Lady Madonna?

"He'd have to be a man, and he'd have to be black," she contemplated. "Prince: that would be cool. We're on the same label [Warner Brothers Records]. Other than that, I'm not interested. There are not that many singers I'm really crazy about."

"So no duet with Julio Iglesias?" I prodded.

"No, but I'll take one of those little boys from Menudo," she countered. "One of the over-the-hill guys, one of the guys they throw out when they get too old!"

"What kind of food do you like?" I asked.

"Japanese," she replied, "and I love to read and go to movies. I hate science fiction, so everything but that. And I hate those Indiana Jones type of movies."

What kind of things really bug Madonna? According to her that afternoon, "My father has this habit of giving old high school boyfriends of mine my phone number in New York. I could kill him. I get phone calls from these guys. 'Remember me? We went out in tenth grade?' I go, 'No! I DON'T remember you!' They want to visit me and find out everything about my life. They're strangers!"

"Are you in touch with anyone from then?" I inquired.

"High school, no. College, definitely," she answered. "I met this guy in Ann Arbor [Steve Bray] who I still write songs with. He played in bands with me, and we've kept in touch. We're like best friends."

Speaking of boyfriends, how did Madonna meet John "Jellybean" Benitez?

"At the DJ booth at The Fun House [a disco on West Twenty-sixth Street]," she recalled. "One of the promotion people from my record company was taking me around to clubs and introducing me to the DJs when my first record was out, and they brought me to The Fun House. And I didn't like him right away. Like, tacky! He had really long hair and was walking around in really short shorts. I thought he was a girl at first. He has a really pretty face—feminine features. Jellybean? Who's that? That doesn't have a sex! Then I ran into him again at a show at The Ritz. Vanity was playing with the Time. Then I knew he wasn't a girl. He started dragging me around everywhere, introducing me to all those industry people. I liked the way he held my hand. That changed my mind—he wasn't such a wimp anymore."

What lies in the future for Madonna? That's something that I was curious about that afternoon in October. What exactly was her overall career game plan? Did she plan on continuing to live in New York City?

"For the next five years," she thought aloud, "I think. I never thought I'd be getting weary of New York, but the buildings are really starting to look ugly."

"See yourself moving to California?" I queried, with the knowledge that she wants to get more involved in a movie career.

"Never permanently," she replied, "but I'd like to get a house in the hills—a real Hollywood house. There's one that belonged to either Anna Pavlova or Isadora Duncan. I want that house! It's on top of a hill, and it's very dramatic. I don't know if anyone lives in it."

"Where do you see yourself ten years from now?" I asked.

"At the Betty Ford Hospital!" she cracked. "It's where all the famous people go. I don't know. It's human nature. People build you up and they tear you down. But I plan to be successful for a long time."

Whatever Madonna wants, Madonna gets. It was evident to me that afternoon that she is totally in control of her own fate. Long-term success for Madonna isn't just another bauble for her charm bracelet—it is destined to become a way of life!

9

Desperately Seeking Susan

MADONNA'S TRANSITION TO the status of movie star has officially taken place, due to the success of the offbeat comedy film *Desperately Seeking Susan*. Together with co-stars Rosanna Arguette, Aidan Quinn, and Robert Joy, she brings to the screen a story of four people whose lives are turned upside down due to an affair being carried on through the personals column of a New York newspaper.

Filmed on location in New York City and in New Jersey during September, October, and November 1984, *Desperately Seeking Susan* is not only being heralded as Madonna's first principal starring role, but it is also the first major film directed by Susan Seidelman.

Desperately Seeking Susan is already being heralded as a box-office hit, but when I first heard about the project, it was still a work-in-progress. It was just a

couple of weeks after my initial interview with Madonna that I visited her on the set of the film. It was a
cold but clear day in Harlem. Into my tape recorder I
made the following spoken notes:

It is eleven-thirty A.M., October 25, 1984. I'm
standing on the corner of 166th Street and St.
Nicholas Avenue with my trusty photographer,
Roger Glazer. Madonna is in her trailer applying
bright orange lipstick to her lips to match her
orange top and headband. She is about ready to
come out to shoot her first scene of the day.

The area is surrounded by police officers, and
we're standing outside the Audubon Ballroom.
It's a bright, sunny day, perfect for filming. A
production crew scurries about, finishing the
scene that precedes Madonna's.

There is all sorts of sound and lighting equip-
ment strapped to the top of an All City yellow
taxicab. Inside the cab are two passengers—a
soundman crouched down on the floor of the
backseat, and in the front seat are two cameramen and a driver.

When Madonna came out of her trailer, she
spent a lot of time sitting in a director's chair,
running lines with Anna Levine, who does a
scene with her outside ''The Magic Club.'' They
ran their lines a couple of times and then sat
around and waited while the cameramen reshot
the taxi sequence.

It is noon, and Madonna's scene has been
pushed back to beyond the lunch break, but she
patiently sits on the set in full makeup. Reid Ros-

efelt took Roger and me on a tour of the rest of the set, upstairs in the ballroom. They've converted this massive two-story ballroom into the Magic Club interior, and Rosanna Arquette's apartment. Reid informed me that this ballroom is the site where Malcolm X was assassinated.

It's approximately ten minutes to one in the afternoon, and Madonna has been brought out of her trailer to finally begin her shots. Now I understand what she meant about waiting around on the set. The set is lit, and the cameras have been loaded. Across the street the sidewalk is lined with an assortment of curious onlookers.

Madonna is wearing ankle-high black boots with high heels and silver rhinestones all over them. She has on fluorescent orange socks, and the tops of her boots are folded down to reveal a lace pattern on the inside. She wears black gloves, a wrist radio, and her signature outrageous jewelry in shades of black. A black rubber crucifix is dangling from her right earlobe. A huge silver five-pointed star is pinned to her bright orange headband. She is wearing dark sunglasses, and she is clearly portraying her greatest role: movie star!

According to Madonna, this waiting around for shots to begin was the only aspect of filmmaking that she wasn't crazy about, but she dealt with it like a trouper. "I'm a really hyperactive person," she explains. "I hate sitting around more than anything. And so many times they make you get up at five in the morning, and they won't use you until after lunch. It's so frustrating, 'cause you can't get mad at them. They'll just say, 'Well, that's making movies!' It's so unpredictable. The weather changes, the sun changes, they have technical difficulties. There are just so many elements involved that really just take time. In records and in videos, I control everything. I decide when to start, I decide who I work with, I decide the studio we work in. In videos I decide—to me, it's all centered around me. I have total control. Here I'm just the actress.''

What does she do to occupy her time on the set? Says La Madonna, "I study my lines in my trailer every morning when I get here. What I usually do at night is go to Rosanna's hotel and talk about boys. Make phone calls. Eat. Stuff like that, just gossip. Anything but think about what we have to do the next day.''

However, she is quick to admit, "It's important to me because I intend to have a career as an actress as well as a singer, and I gotta start somewhere. This is a very good first project for me, and so it's important to me. It's important to be good, and this is the right time, so everything just seems right about it.''

Of the script memorization process, she proclaims, "Memorization is really easy; it's integrating it into the actual scene and really feeling it that's hard. You have to forget about the lines so it sounds like you're just saying them.''

While at work on the movie, Madonna became very close friends with Rosanna Arquette, who first found fame in her film roles in *Executioner's Song* and *Baby, It's You*. According to Madonna, "We're like sisters. We've got lots of miseries in common, and boyfriend problems." Adds Rosanna, "I love her. She's my long-lost sister!"

On November 29, 1984, I interviewed Susan Seidelman about her new film and about Madonna. The interview took place in Seidelman's SoHo loft, and she confirmed my suspicions that Madonna was going to cause quite a sensation on the screen. Seidelman, thirty-one, first found fame by producing and directing a cult film titled *Smithereens*. The first draft of the script for *Desperately Seeking Susan* was shown to her in 1982 when she was touring the world to promote *Smithereens*.

Susan and I discussed recording stars becoming film stars, her future projects, and her predictions about Madonna's future.

MARK: How did you get involved in this film?

SUSAN: I was reading screenplays while I was traveling. At some point I had read the screenplay for *Desperately Seeking Susan*, and it just appealed to me. First of all, I liked the title.

MARK: It's a catchy title.

SUSAN: Yes, and I liked the idea of the story that one woman takes over another woman's identity, and the fact that they are two very different kinds of women.

MARK: Did you come up with the ideas for the casting?

SUSAN: Well, Rosanna was one of . . . Well, the producers and I had talked about using Rosanna, and she sort of was involved in an early stage of the project, so she was kind of the given star. When Orion decided to do the movie, they knew that it was going to be this script, me as the director, and Rosanna as the star.

MARK: Was she under contract to Orion?

SUSAN: No contract. She had just read the script in an earlier stage, liked it, and said, "If someone wants to make this movie, I want to be in it." And then we were looking for somebody to play Susan. I knew of Madonna for a couple of years, just from sort of . . .

MARK: The New York music scene?

SUSAN: Exactly. She was beginning to get popular, but it was only in the last month or two that she's really become such a phenomenon. So I kept seeing her face when I read the script, as Susan. She seemed like an exciting choice. And I think at first the producers and the studio people were a little nervous, because . . .

MARK: She didn't have any real acting credits, did she?

SUSAN: No, and the character she's playing—it isn't a rock-and-roll part. It isn't like Prince. You know, just get up there, have her sing . . .

MARK: . . . and be Madonna.

SUSAN: It's an acting role; it's not a singing role. So they were pretty set on finding an actress who could play that kind of a part, but there was something about Madonna. I think it's just kind of her . . . She's got a sort of a bad girl/good girl quality that I think is real interesting. She's a little tough, but not too tough. A little "street," but also, I think, real appealing. Earthy in a way that I thought was essential to the character. And I didn't want to get an actress who was going to try to . . .

MARK: . . . turn into something that they're not?

SUSAN: Yes, put on clothes and sort of a make-believe street attitude.

MARK: Yeah, like Margaux Hemingway doing it, or someone who just wasn't the part.

SUSAN: Yeah, Margaux Hemingway in Spandex! I thought that Madonna had a sort of authentic quality that would be really good to try to capture on film. I was a little nervous myself, because there was a lot of dialogue in the script, and I just didn't know how well she'd do. But I had seen her in her videos. She's a performer. I think that if she can perform on video, she can perform on film. Once she had the confidence to allow herself to be uninhibited on film, she's wonderful. There's a presence. You know, you can get great actors, but some people just have an aura about them that you can't learn in acting school. And I think that she's got that. And she turned out as good as I hoped she would be. She's really quite good in the film.

MARK: So you think that you've come up with a successful product with her in the role?

SUSAN: Yes, I think she's going to be a movie star!

MARK: I can see this happening to her. It's amazing all the things that she has going at the moment.

SUSAN: Other people . . . I actually wasn't as nervous about this, but some people thought, "Rock stars are really prima donnas" or whatever. She wasn't. She was actually a pleasure to work with. She listened to feedback. If you made a suggestion, she would try to incorporate that into what she did.

MARK: She didn't have the "diva" attitude?

SUSAN: I don't think she did at all.

MARK: So basically, you've really helped her movie career get under way.

SUSAN: I hope so. I saw a rough cut of the film last night for the first time, all put together. I think that it's charming. I think that there's something there—knock on wood. Because, who knows? You can't predict what's going to be successful and what's not, but I think that everyone did a good job.

MARK: A lot of the clothes that I saw on the set looked like they could have come out of Madonna's own closet. I had to assume that she brought a lot of her own fashion sense to the part.

SUSAN: Well, she did. I think that she's got a great sense of style.

MARK: Oh, yes! Everyone seems to be emulating what she's doing with her jewelry and clothes.

"LIKE A VIRGIN!" Here's MADONNA in her wedding dress and "Boy Toy" belt at the first annual "MTV Awards" at Radio City Music Hall, September 14, 1984. (Photo: Robin Platzer)

Sophomore

Junior

MADONNA as a high school cheerleader: Rochester Adams High School, Rochester, Michigan; 1973.

MADONNA's high school yearbook

(Photos: the archives of Mark James Brooky)

Senior

LEFT: MADONNA (second from the upper left) and the girls greet the visiting cheerleaders.

ABOVE: MADONNA (top row, right side) and the squad in full formation.

ABOVE: MADONNA and JOHN "JELLYBEAN" BENITEZ, enjoying a night on the town at Private Eyes, N.Y.C. (Photo: Robin Platzer)

THEY WEAR THEIR sunglasses at night! MADONNA and GRACE JONES at the opening of the N.Y.C. video club Private Eyes, summer 1984. (Photo: Robin Platzer)

ABOVE: MADONNA and ROSANNA ARQUETTE celebrate their on-screen "victory" at Private Eyes, autumn 1984. (Photo: Robin Platzer)

DAVID LEE ROTH of the group Van Halen, and MADONNA, having a couple of laughs at the Manhattan club Area. (Photo: Robin Platzer)

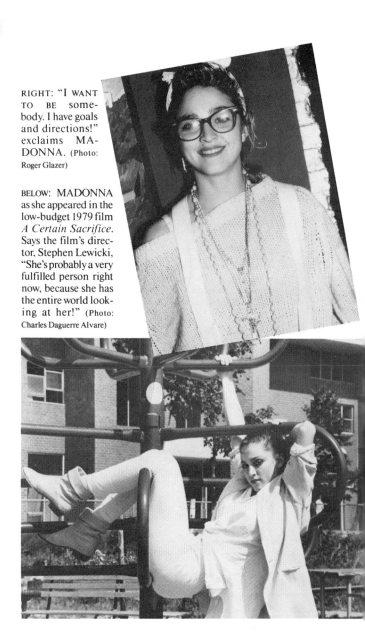

RIGHT: "I WANT TO BE somebody. I have goals and directions!" exclaims MADONNA. (Photo: Roger Glazer)

BELOW: MADONNA as she appeared in the low-budget 1979 film *A Certain Sacrifice*. Says the film's director, Stephen Lewicki, "She's probably a very fulfilled person right now, because she has the entire world looking at her!" (Photo: Charles Daguerre Alvare)

ABOVE: MADONNA: Our Lady of Rock Video! (Photo: Roger Glazer)

LEFT: "SUSAN'S A REAL adventurer; she's carefree, she's irresponsible—kind of like me!" says MADONNA. (Photo: Andy Schwartz for Orion Pictures)

RIGHT: DESPERATELY SEEKING jewelry! MA-DONNA brings a bit of her own fashion sense to Susan's character. (Photo: Andy Schwartz for Orion Pictures)

MADONNA and *Desperately Seeking Susan* director SUSAN SEIDELMAN in midproduction. Says Seidelman of Madonna, "She's got a good girl/bad girl quality that I think is interesting. I think that she is going to be a movie star!" (Photo: Andy Schwartz for Orion Pictures)

LEFT: MADONNA explains her next scene to author MARK BEGO on the set of *Desperately Seeking Susan.* (Photo: Roger Glazer)

Movie star MADONNA on the set of *Desperately Seeking Susan,* October 1984. (Photo: Roger Glazer)

RIGHT: "We're like sisters!" says MADONNA of her *Desperately Seeking Susan* co-star ROSANNA ARQUETTE (left). (Photo: Andy Schwartz for Orion Pictures)

BELOW: Jailhouse rock! MADONNA as Susan—a diva behind bars! (Photo: Andy Schwartz for Orion Pictures)

"During high school, I became slightly schizophrenic," explains MADONNA. "I couldn't choose between class virgin or the other kind!" (Photo: Robin Platzer)

BELOW: HUEY LEWIS and MADONNA make" the news," as they present a trophy at the American Music Awards, Shrine Auditorium in Los Angeles, January 28, 1985. (Photo: Scott Downie)

ABOVE: MADONNA looking luscious in leather the night of the American Music Awards, January 1985. (Photo: Scott Downie)

RIGHT: "It comes down to doing what you have to do for your career," MADONNA proclaims. "You want it, you find a way to get it!" (Photo: Scott Downie)

LEFT: A "material girl" makes her mark in the movies! MADONNA checks out the personals column of the newspaper as "desperately sought-after" Susan. In real life she MAKES the headlines instead of reading them! (Photo: Andy Schwartz for Orion Pictures)

BELOW: "I've always worn crucifixes," claims MADONNA. "There's something very mysterious and alluring about it." (Photo: Scott Downie)

MADONNA belts out the song "Gambler" from the film *Vision Quest*. This scene was shot in a club in the fall of 1983 in Spokane, Washington.

LEFT: MADONNA LOU-
ISE CICCONE: Is she the
Marilyn Monroe of the
1980s? (Photo: Kate Simon-Star
File)

BELOW: MADONNA and
JELLYBEAN smooch at
the American Music
Awards in L.A., January
28, 1985. Says Jellybean,
"Madonna makes all her
own decisions. No one tells
her what to do." (Photo: Scott
Downie)

According to MADONNA, "My rock-and-roll fashion image is a contradiction. My two favorite fantasies were always a cross between Nancy Sinatra and a nun!" (Photo: Scope Features-RDR)

SUSAN: Yes, it would have been ridiculous to . . .

MARK: . . . tamper with a working formula?

SUSAN: Yeah, really! Or to try to put her in things that felt like a costume, because I don't like when people get into things. Like when I see movies and stuff, and it looks like actresses in hooker clothes. There's something phony about it, the way it looks kind of overly cute or something.

MARK: Like they just went to Frederick's of Hollywood for sleazy lingerie or something.

SUSAN: Exactly.

MARK: Because the scene that I saw her in, and the stills that I've seen as well, she looks very confidently the character, yet Madonna's version of it.

SUSAN: Right.

MARK: Now, in the movie, Rosanna Arquette picks up Madonna's personality, doesn't she?

SUSAN: Yes.

MARK: So does Madonna become a New Jersey housewife?

SUSAN: She doesn't become a New Jersey housewife, but she does end up . . . In the middle of the movie she does bump into Roberta's husband because they're both looking for Roberta—that's the housewife.

MARK: I assumed it was New Jersey, because I know that you shot those scenes there. Is that where it takes place as well?

SUSAN: Yes. And since Madonna doesn't have a place to stay, this guy comes along, and

they both realize that they're both looking
for the same person. She sort of moves
into his house in New Jersey. She doesn't
become a housewife, but she sort of takes
advantage of the things that are there. She
sort of gets off in a "goof" kind of way
on the built-in swimming pool and the
Jacuzzi.

MARK: Could you see yourself working with
           Madonna again?

SUSAN: Sure! I think she's wonderful. Actually, I
           thing she can be very funny. What I think
           would be interesting for her for the next
           thing is to go sort of against type. Not to
           play sort of the sexy vampy type person,
           but to try to do something like Carole
           Lombard-ish. The screwball-comedy
           type thing. She's got the timing. I mean
           she was a dancer. I think she could be real
           funny.

MARK: Are you looking at new scripts already?

SUSAN: Well, I'm starting to read scripts. There's
           something that I've been wanting to do, that
           actually I've been wanting to do before this,
           and that's when I first started thinking about
           Madonna. Because this other project I had,
           I thought Madonna would have been really
           good for. Did you happen to see this thing
           Leader of the Pack at the Bottom Line,
           about Ellie Greenwich?

MARK: No. I heard a lot about it, but I'm sorry that
           I missed it, to tell you the truth. It was kind
           of autobiographical, about her life as a

songwriter. I understand it's coming to Broadway.

SUSAN: Because this was something that I did way before I even heard about that. It was a script I'd worked on with somebody about girl groups from the early sixties. It was actually about the Shangri-las.

MARK: Really?

SUSAN: Yeah. Remember "Walkin' In The Sand"?

MARK: Yeah!

SUSAN: It was about three girls from Queens in 1963 who have a group, and so on and so on. And I thought of Madonna for one of them. Right now I haven't had much time to think about anything but the editing of *Desperately Seeking Susan*. But once I settle down, I want to go back and . . .

MARK: That's great, so you're still considering that script?

SUSAN: Yes, I am.

MARK: I love the girl groups from the sixties.

SUSAN: That whole time was kind of interesting. Did you ever see the videotape *The Girl Groups*?

MARK: Yes! It was marvelous!

SUSAN: I mean, the whole style of that time.

MARK: The Dynel wigs and everything. It really is kind of a time capsule unto itself. So that's something that you might be working with Madonna on?

SUSAN: Yeah, it's something that just appeals to me. I'm just getting nervous because *Smithereens* had a rock-and-roll element.

This movie doesn't have a rock-and-roll
element, but it has Madonna. Part of me
wants to do it. Part of me is afraid of getting
pegged as a . . .

MARK: . . . rock-and-roll director?

SUSAN: Yes, although the story would be about
growing up in Queens with these girls, and
it's not going to be like *Purple Rain*.

MARK: You had mentioned that Madonna would be
great in a screwball Carole Lombard type of
comedy. Do you see yourself doing
something like that—a period piece like that
from the 1930s?

SUSAN: Well, I think that *Desperately Seeking
Susan* has certain screwball elements to it in
a contemporary way. Actually, it's not the
Madonna character [who's like] ''Lucy,''
but Rosanna Arquette is a little bit Lucille
Ball-ish in this movie.

MARK: I just saw Linda Ronstadt doing *La Boheme*
with Gary Morris and really liked it. Do
you feel that pop culture and films are
becoming more closely meshed? Suddenly
people like Linda Ronstadt and Prince and
Madonna are getting involved in movies
and theater. What's your opinion of where
pop performers are going?

SUSAN: I think that's good! I'm not an elitist about
film at all. I grew up on Doris Day and
Hayley Mills movies. I love it. Natalie
Wood was my idol as a kid. In fact, the first
time I had seen foreign films I was already
in college. I really didn't know from that.

MARK: Do you think that the pop-music world is
        getting justifiably more involved in film?

SUSAN: You can't deny its impact. The elitists,
        whatever field they're in, whether it's
        classical music or whatever—if you're an
        artist and you want to deal with something
        about life, you cannot deny the influence of
        pop culture on contemporary life.

MARK: Do you think that realism in films has been
        taken too far? Is romanticism coming back
        on the screen?

SUSAN: We're getting to a less realistic stage, even
        with fashion. If you look at fashion and
        stuff, the sort of natural look is out. People
        are dressing up more. Look at Madonna's
        stuff. She wears lace-seamed black bras and
        all that other kind of stuff which is totally
        out of the fifties *film noir, femme fatale*
        kind of thing!

As the unit publicist for *Desperately Seeking Susan*,
Reid Rosefelt was in charge of alerting the media
about the progress of the production, lining up interviews with members of the cast and crew, and distributing the photographic stills to magazines and
newspapers. One of the first things that Reid was responsible for was for compiling the production notes to
be circulated to the press. While compiling information about the cast, he got to know everyone involved
from the very beginning stages of the film.

Having worked on the prestigious Cannes Film Fes-
tival, as well as with Susan Seidelman on *Smithereens*,
Reid is extremely well-versed in the behind-the-scenes

world of the movie industry. When I interviewed him
on January 30, 1985, he drew his opinions from his
day-to-day observations on the set. Here's what he had
to say about Madonna and her professional acting debut.

MARK: As far as your dealings with Madonna,
         when did you first meet her?
REID: I met her at the production office. I was
         starting to put together the press book
         which was being distributed to the press
         while the film was being shot. I was
         immediately impressed with her because
         she had so much charisma. I had only seen
         her videos; I guess very few people have
         seen her perform. She just had so much
         charisma, and I had only been reading the
         script of this character Susan. I remember
         after I met her, I just asked her a few
         questions and probably talked to her for all
         of two minutes. I went and called up Susan
         Seidelman and told her about how perfect
         she was for the part. I thought that she'd
         made a really good choice.
MARK: So in other words, she matched the
         description of the character?
REID: She had "attitude."
MARK: [laughing] That's Madonna!
REID: The character does too! So she has to be the
         kind of person who can talk her way in and
         out of anything. And immediately I knew
         that Madonna was somebody important,
         just from meeting her just for a second.

MARK: A lot of people are put off by her attitude. They think that she's kind of cool. Did that pose any problems, working with her?

REID: I liked her. She has a sense of humor. She's cool, but there's also a kind of wink in it as well, and I've worked with a lot of people like that before, and I wasn't surprised by it. And I figured that if she acted like that, that she wasn't really serious. I think that some people can meet her for one meeting for a half hour, and they can get the wrong idea. When we finished up publicity, Madonna gave me a poster, and she signed it, and she said: "To Reid: You've been a real pain in the ass. Thanks a lot!— Madonna." So, I mean that sort of sums up the whole thing.

MARK: Yeah, kind of tongue-in-cheek sort of sense of humor. As the film progressed, you saw a lot of the film as it was happening. This was really her first dramatic film role. How was she? Did she start out slowly getting into it, or did she just dive in knowing exactly what to do?

REID: She really dived in. I thought she was good. The change that I think was made was just her manner on the set. By the time we were shooting some of the last scenes in the film, she was like an old trouper. She was picking up the clapper board and making jokes, and she was very relaxed with the whole idea. I was there when she did her first shot in the movie, and she didn't seem particularly nervous or anything in front of the camera. She just went out and did it.

MARK: So she really took to it?

REID: She took to it right away. I think it was . . . Obviously acting in a movie for the first time is a learning experience, and she was watching what was going on. I think she got very close with Rosanna Arquette, and I think they shared things and they talked about things. But she'd been a performer for a long time, and she'd acted in school plays in high school, and there was a sense that this was something that she'd been planning on doing for a long time, even if it was the first time.

MARK: So she was a natural for film?

REID: Yes.

MARK: And did a majority of the people get along with her on the set?

REID: Yes. She's very professional. She was always there when she had to be there, and I think when people are talking about hiring somebody from the world of rock and roll for a movie . . .

MARK: They probably have a lot of skepticism about it, I bet!

REID: Yeah, they don't believe that they ever go to sleep, or they're always at parties or something like that. But that's not the case with Madonna. She was really dedicated and a real pro all the way.

MARK: Did she bring any of her own personal ideas

to the script or the wardrobe, or anything
that she made creative suggestions on?

REID: Well, Santo Loquasto was the designer of
the costumes, as well as the production
designer for the whole film. He's worked
with Woody Allen; he won an Oscar
nomination for *Zelig* and a Tony award for
The Cherry Orchard. So he's a very big guy
in the design world. He knows what he's
doing. His vision of the character was much
more West Side old clothes and thrift-shop,
which is not Madonna's look at all. He
went up to Madonna's place and looked
through her things, and I think there was a
kind of give and take between what Santo
wanted, what Madonna wanted, and what
the plot needed, what Susan Seidelman
needed. I mean, there are certain clothes,
there's a pair of boots which are very
important to the plot.

MARK: You mean the ones with the rhinestones?

REID: Yeah, they're like glitter boots, and that's a
very important part of the story of the film.
And I think that those might not be boots
that Madonna would want to wear, but they
looked very good on film. Certain things
had to be worked out. It was a mutual
discussion. When you see the film, you'll
see that a lot of the look . . . She's wearing
a lot of her own stuff, because Susan has a
lot of crucifixes on, and a lot of jewelry that
in a large part, these are Madonna's own
clothes.

MARK: Maripol, Madonna's jewelry designer,
          wasn't actively on the set, was she?

REID: No, I never saw her. She might have
          visited.

MARK: These are things that sound like a lot of
          Maripol's designs.

REID: Yes, definitely, these are a lot of Maripol's
          designs.

MARK: Where do you think that Madonna is going
          to go from here? What do you think this
          movie is going to mean for her career?

REID: I think that it will show that she can act as
          well, and there's a lot of projects that
          people are preparing for her now. I think
          that this should . . . They're probably
          taking a look. A lot of them are probably
          waiting to see how this one comes out. I
          think it's going to get her going for a film
          career.

MARK: There have been many correlations between
          Madonna and many different movie stars of
          the past. Susan Seidelman said that she's
          very much like Carole Lombard, and she
          could see her doing Carole Lombard type of
          comedies. And then a lot of people have
          called her the 1980s version of Marilyn
          Monroe, and of course the "Material Girl"
          video blatantly makes that imagery clear.
          How do you think that she fits in with that
          blond sex goddess image. I mean, she's
          clearly not a blond bimbo, but there is a
          comic timing that those ladies all had.

REID: I think that when people get to know her

well, they're going to see that there's a bit of Mae West in her. She's a hell of a lot better looking than Mae West, but she's got a sense of humor, there's a tartness, she's sharp with . . . You could throw Judy Holliday in there too! I think that people are just getting to know Madonna, at least what she's got to offer as a performer.

MARK: Do you think that the film is going to be important for her?

REID: I do. But it's just the beginning.

MARK: Is Susan Seidelman planning on doing other projects with Madonna?

REID: I don't know, and I'm sure that her career is going to have a lot to do with this film. I don't think that as of now. No deals have been made yet.

MARK: Was *Desperately Seeking Susan* shot in sequence?

REID: No, it was shot totally out of sequence. In fact, Madonna's first scene in the movie was the last scene that was shot. It takes place in an Atlantic City hotel. In the movie she wakes up, and she's in this hotel, and Richard Hell is sleeping in the bed, and she is going through his stuff, and she sort of kisses him good-bye, and takes off. That's the first time you see her in the movie. And that was the last scene that we shot of principal photography. There were some things like inserts that were shot after that, but that was the last day everybody was on the set.

MARK: Do you think that this film is going to be as important to Madonna as *Purple Rain* was to Prince?

REID: *Purple Rain* was what you would call a "vehicle." It was made around Prince's personality. This was a part that Madonna could look at and say, "I could play that!" And she could find things in her personality that could fit that, but that's not her. Susan's not Madonna. I guess that Prince may argue that he's really not that character, but it really wasn't working [as an actor]. They began with the idea of doing something which would be good for Prince. When they make a movie which is a vehicle for Madonna, which is being worked on, many projects where people are going to say, "This is what she can do, and we're going to work with that," it will obviously show her off much more than this. This is a film which she plays one part in. Rosanna Arquette has parts. It's not [Madonna's] film; there are many other characters.

MARK: Do you think that *Desperately Seeking Susan* will make Hollywood take Madonna more seriously than Prince? I mean, I can't see Prince doing a dramatic role!

REID: Yeah, I think so. I think people will say, "She can play parts." She can do lots of things, and it wouldn't have to be a musical necessarily. This isn't a musical. Would they put Prince in a movie if he wasn't singing in it?

MARK: I can't imagine it.

REID: It's like Sting, for example. He plays parts, and now he's acting opposite Meryl Streep. I think it's more like that than *Purple Rain*.

MARK: What would a regular day on the set involve for Madonna?

REID: Really what she did, she came in, she did her makeup, she looked at her lines, and she came out there and she did her scenes over and over again, and it was really like that. As a press agent for the film, I was just really watching like everyone else.

MARK: Other than that, it was pretty routine?

REID: It was fun! There were a lot of laughs, and she had the capacity to make jokes. There was a looseness about her sometimes. She'd be having fun with the other people, playing around and stuff like that. I admired her, and I liked her, and I was really glad that she was cast in the part. It was fun working with her.

One thing that she said to me that I put in my press book on her is, she said, "1985 is going to be my year, you watch!"

When Madonna was busy on the set of *Desperately Seeking Susan*, she knew that big things were right around the bend for her. Principal photography for the film was completed in the beginning of November, and only days later one of the fastest selling albums of the decade was released: *Like A Virgin*.

10

"Like A Virgin"

THE FALL OF 1984 BELONGED to Madonna. Beginning with her controversial performance on the first annual "MTV Awards" program, she racked up one accolade after another. After a year on the charts, her debut album *Madonna*, cracked the top ten after selling over two million copies, and her fifth single, "Lucky Star," hit number four on the pop charts.

Now, at long last, the time was right for the release of Madonna's second album, *Like A Virgin*. When I heard the song "Like A Virgin" on the "MTV Awards" show in September, I knew that it was a number-one hit, and I was one hundred percent right. Both the single and the album became two of the fastest selling records in the history of Warner Brothers Records.

Debuting on the *Billboard* chart at an astonishing number forty-eight the week of November 17, 1984, the single cracked the top ten four weeks later at number three, and the next week (December 22, 1984) was the number-one record in America. Even quicker than that, "Like A Virgin" topped the Australian singles charts the week of December 10, 1984! The song and the album were also huge top-ten successes in Britain, Canada, West Germany, Holland, Italy, and Japan! Madonna had officially conquered the world—and that was just the beginning.

In America the "Like A Virgin" single stayed on top of the charts for six solid weeks. The week of February 9, 1985, Madonna's *Like A Virgin* album knocked Prince and Bruce Springsteen out of the way to become a number-one smash. She entered the charts like a virgin and emerged a platinum-plated professional. Madonna's album sold as many copies in ten weeks as Cyndi Lauper's *She's So Unusual* album sold in a year! Madonna was now the fastest selling female artist on the charts. Not even Tina Turner and her stellar *Private Dancer* album sold as many copies! 1985 was clearly destined to become The Year of Madonna!

As though gimmicks were necessary, the promotional copies of the album that went out to DJs and music-media journalists like myself were pressed on "Like A Virgin" *white* vinyl! If you can get hold of one of those, it's a real collector's item.

On November 7, 1984, Warner Brothers Records threw a party for Madonna and her new album at the high-tech video rock club Private Eyes (12 West Twenty-first Street). It was at that party that I first feasted my eyes on Madonna's exotic video version of "Like A Virgin," and to see it for the initial viewing on the club's large screen was a real rush! It looked great blown-up larger than life.

There in the middle of all the excitement was Madonna herself, looking very nonchalant. Pausing in the middle of her conversation with Andy Warhol, Madonna waved and acknowledged me by saying, "Hello, Mark." That was the extent of our conversation. She was clearly holding court that evening, and rightfully so—this was her first official outing as the new undisputed Princess of Pop Music.

Let's Get Critical

The music critics jumped on Madonna's *Like A Virgin* album. Some of the reviews were favorable, and some of the reviews were decidedly critical—as though it mattered. Once the record-buying public heard *Like A Virgin*, no obscure acid-penned record scribe could dissuade a determined buying public.

Here's what the major media outlets had to say about the *Like A Virgin* LP:

Cashbox—". . . produced by veteran funk/ rocker Nile Rodgers, *Like A Virgin* elaborates on the singer's sex kitten image with such teasers as 'Dress You Up' and 'Pretender' while displaying Madonna's more serious side on 'Over And Over' and 'Stay.'. . . a healthy dose of disco/rock."

Rolling Stone—". . . Despite her little-girl voice, there's an undercurrent of ambition that makes her more than the latest Betty Boop. . . . Rodgers wisely supplies the kind of muscle Madonna's sassy lyrics demand. Her light voice bobs over the heavy rhythm and synth tracks like a kid on a carnival ride. . . . She knows what works on the dance floor. . . . Madonna's a lot more interesting as a conniving cookie, flirting her way to the top, than as a bummed-out adult.''

19—''Virgin on the Ridiculous! . . . Madonna's second album—under the pun-in-cheek title *Like A Virgin*—wasn't the funkier, less-controlled piece of work she's earlier promised. Offering less verve and more smooch, as it does, it's a bit disappointing.''

Billboard—''. . . a fevered dance-rock momentum. . . . This second album brings considerable muscle to the equation, thanks to producer Nile Rodgers' sleek but sinewy rhythm arrangements, burnished to surgical sharpness by crisp digital sonics.''

People—''. . . A practitioner of lingerie rock . . . Madonna Louise Ciccone does have a sense of humor, though, even if, like her sister singers of the Cyndi Lauper school, she is buried under so many layers of self-parody it's hard to tell sometimes. . . . A tolerable bit of fluff.''

Record—''. . . brilliantly produced and arranged.

. . . She's turned out to be a spunky beat-conscious sex kitten instead of a disco pet. . . . Tailored to let her kick up her heels like a hip hop Marilyn Monroe. . . . A celebration of ambition . . . it should keep Madonna dancing all over the airwaves for a long time.''

Us—". . . delectable . . . addictive. . . . Madonna is perfect for lighter-than-air songs. . . . Madonna's not a 'virgin' anymore—this is her second album—but she's up to her old tricks, and in this case, 'more of the same' is just fine.''

Nile Rodgers

A very large degree of the credit for the success of Madonna's *Like A Virgin* album has to go to the producer that she so wisely chose to handle the project. Nile's track record is widely strewn with gold.

Having first hit the crest of the music scene as one-half of the brains behind the million-selling disco hit-makers who called themselves Chic, Nile has gone on to become one of THE hottest record producers of the decade. His track record includes such gems as David Bowie's "Let's Dance," Duran Duran's "Wild Boys," Diana Ross' "I'm Coming Out," and one of my all-time favorites, Debby Harry's *Koo Koo* album.

Madonna proclaims that Nile "is a very passionate man. He lives life to the hilt. When you deal with people who are that way, you get good stuff and bad stuff, but it was really great working with him." Well, this time around, Madonna went to Nile and got outrageously phenomenal stuff!

Nile returns the compliments, although there were all kinds of rumors flying about, claiming that Madonna could be a real "bitch" to work with in the recording studio. Says Rodgers of La Madonna, "She's fantastic, one of my favorite people in the world! She's a really incredible artist, she really knows what she wants, and we just do it together, we work great as a team. That's like a marriage made in heaven.

"She didn't stumble across her success," continues Nile. "She knows what she's doing." But he admits, "She's more temperamental than anyone I've ever worked with, but I probably needed someone like that because it helped me learn how to deal with that sort of thing. It's not a bad thing at all. Some people do it and it's a drag, because they don't have the talent to back it up, but when Madonna does it, it's because something's really bothering her, and she says, 'Oh, Nile, come on. That guitar sound sucks!' You know she really means that!" Madonna assuredly isn't one to mince words.

"What I did was try to make it sound good—sound authentic with a new edge," explains Rodgers of his approach to Madonna's second LP. One of the technical changes that he made on the sound was to use a live drummer, as opposed to the drum machines that Reggie Lucas, Mark Kamins, and Jellybean used on the *Madonna* album. Explains Nile, "The reason why I wanted to use Tony Thompson (former drummer with Chic) was, to me it seemed really important for Madonna to have just a little more musical credibility, just a little more artistry, because when you're dealing with songs that have the subject matter of Madonna's songs, critics tend to say that they're really weak, so you go for every little thing that you can spot to get into. If you overdid the drum machines and stuff like that with an artist like Madonna, it starts to become a little bubble-gummy, whereas Eurythmics, because their subject matter is usually a little bit more political or ostensibly heavier, let's say, can do that, and it sounds great when they do it. Then it's Art, you know, it's dynamite! But with someone like Madonna, who's talking about, you know, a boy that she met last night and the way that he dresses, and his hair is like this, and his teeth are pearly white, and 'Boy, I sure wish I could go home with him in his car!'—basically, one would say that they're incredibly frivolous songs, in the scope of the world. I mean, it's not like she's singing about famine in Ethiopia or politics in South Africa. I mean, that's not what her music is about.''

Adds Nile, ''I think the reason I was able to work very, very well with Madonna is that's really what Chic was about, and in a way that's sort of my personal philosophy. I keep my politics in a more political arena or to myself. And my music is something else! It makes me have a good time.'' Whatever the underlying motivation behind the tracks, the music that resulted from the talents of Nile as producer and Madonna as artist was a runaway smash! *Like A Virgin* is destined to become one of the albums that defines the decade of the 1980s.

The *Like A Virgin* Album

Side one of the LP begins with the brilliant "Material Girl," setting off the disk's mood with a pulsing pastiche of a song—part "Diamonds Are A Girl's Best Friend," part bourgeois eighties anthem, and one hundred percent Madonna. Composed by Peter Brown and Robert Rans, the song is so peppy and fun it was destined to become a number-one smash before it was even pressed as a single. Bernard Edward's infectious bass line, and the use of male background singers pump out a pop classic. With Madonna's undefinable yelps and petulant bratty attitude, the effect is magical.

"Angel," the cut that follows, is a medium-paced rock ballad, punctuated with Madonna's frothy and girlish giggling. "Oooh, you're an angel," she insists in this confectionary composition by Madonna and Steve Bray. The pleading vocal arrangement is the perfect follow-up cut to the blatantly hard-hitting "Material Girl." Light, but not too light. Nile's signature bass-dominated production moves the song along with perfect results.

The title cut of the album is next on the program. "Like A Virgin" was written by Billy Steinberg and Tom Kelly, and the very idea of the song being sung by a girl named Madonna was just outrageous enough a "hook" to make it an instant smash. The musical arrangement is crisp and clear as a bell, and the perfect distillation of guitar, bass, drum, and synthesizers. Again the bass line keeps the song chugging along, and Madonna's sharp but lilting voice keeps the cut lively, while her giddy "heeeee's" make the song tongue-in-cheek fun.

The pace picks up a bit for "Over And Over," a fast number about the Madonna philosophy of life. Pick a goal and go for it, is the message, convincingly stated by the insistent Ms. Ciccone. The song was composed by Madonna and Steve Bray and has obvious hit-single potential as well.

The first side of the album ends with Madonna's first ballad release: "Love Don't Live Here Anymore." The song had been a hit for the short-lived group Rose Royce (remember "Car Wash"?) and I was excited to see that the long-lost tune had been updated by Madonna. This is the song that a lot of the critics jumped on with knives, but I rather like this string-laden change of pace. Madonna's vocal approach is breathy and torchy and a fine outlet for her to stretch out and show another side of her vocal persona. According to Madonna herself, "I don't want to have all positive songs or just maudlin, depressing songs. I just wanted to show different sides of my personality." I think that this song serves as a fine showcase for just that. The song was written by Miles Gregory.

Side two of the album opens with another high-powered hit titled "Dress You Up." Written by Peggy Stanziale and Andrea LaRusso, the cut is a great dreamy girl's song about outfitting a lover in "love." Nile throws in a great guitar solo midsong, while the ever-present beat and ethereal background chorus shoot the sound heavenward. A surefire smash from the word go!

The next cut, "Shoo-Bee-Doo," is another ballad outing, this time around composed by Madonna herself. The music is dreamy, and Madonna's vocals are direct and controlled throughout. A tasty sax solo in the middle of the mix gives the song a jazzy touch.

Drumbeats begin "Pretender," which is a medium-tempo Motown-flavor cut written by Madonna and Steve Bray. In the lyrics we find Madonna kicking herself for falling in love with a phony. The cut is subtle, pleasant, and the type of song that doesn't grab you right off the bat, but grows on you.

The album ends with a harder-hitting cut, "Stay." The Nile Rodgers sound is ever-present on this rhythmic uptempo tune. Another Madonna/Steve Bray composition, the pleading lead and doo-wop background vocals drive the cut home with a rocking beat.

All in all, *Like A Virgin* is a shimmering success. Not only does it define and refine Madonna's tough-as-nails gold digger image, but it shows off her multi-format versatility. *Madonna* made her a star, but *Like A Virgin* put her into the superstar category. Bravo, Niles—and congrats, Madonna!

The "Jellybean" Mix

When I interviewed John "Jellybean" Benitez in November 1984 for a magazine article I was working on, he explained to me how he changed the album version of Madonna's "Like A Virgin" from an upbeat three-minute-and-fifty-six second cut, into a hard-hitting number-one dance track of six minutes and seven seconds. The Jellybean mix, by the way, is available commercially as an "extended dance mix."

Anyway, according to Jellybean, "I listened to the track. It was done by a real drummer. It was strange because the drummer didn't play the same drum pattern all the way through. The tempo changed a lot. I don't know what he was thinking about when he did it. When you listened to the record as a whole, it sounded fine, but when you broke it down, it was really weird because he didn't play the same patterns. So every time I would do an edit or try to extend a section or change something around, it didn't work. It sounded like your turntable was speeding up or slowing down. The tempo kept changing. It wouldn't work! So it took a really long time to figure that out.

"It really wasn't designed to be a dance record, so all the sections were really short," he continued, "and the tempo changed, so it didn't work. So we did some percussion overdubs. Then we did some synthesizer overdubs on it; and on the choruses, when she goes, 'like a virgin,' we put this bell-sounding synthesizer on it. I felt that the vocal hook was strong, but they needed a more musical hook to them, and in the original production it wasn't done. So I added this bell chord. And on the end, when I took 'Lucky Star'—the end of the song—or is it 'Borderline'? No, 'Borderline,' where she goes, 'Baby, baby, baby,' I kept repeating the word 'baby.' So on 'Like A Virgin' she says 'baby,' and I put it through a series of delay units and a harmonizer, and it has a synthesizer player—play it back—so it gave like a really weird sound. So, toward the end of the song, this really weird sound comes in all of a sudden, and you don't know what it is, and it's Madonna singing through a synthesizer!"

Jellybean further explained his extended mix: "Every time it goes into the chorus, the music underneath comes up for one beat and then goes back in until she says 'virgin,' and then it's really pumping. Then there's a little synthesizer that I added to the beginning of the choruses that sort of lead up to it. There's a lot of echo on the snare drum, right before the down-beat. Everything falls out and she's just singing, 'like a . . .' There's no music underneath—and then she says 'virgin!' It all comes back in.

"It was like putting the pieces of a puzzle to-gether," he said. "Every record's different. You need a good intro, you need a good breakdown, and you need a good outro, and it has to build. I think that part that we put in at the end of 'Like A Virgin' really makes people remember that."

On a personal note, it was about this same time that Madonna's personal relationship with Jellybean began to change, due in part to her huge and growing popu-larity. In that same interview, Jellybean explained part of the phenomenon to me by admitting, "It gets pretty crazy sometimes. People constantly—not clawing at her—but we go to a restaurant and we can't go any-place where she has to sit idle for too long. If we go to a movie, we have to get there just before they let peo-ple in: walk into the theater and get the worst seats. We can't go to Macy's shopping. Things like that, that I never thought about before, have to be considered now. We can't go to a restaurant where it's really bright. We can't just go to any club anymore because we have to be careful of the type of people that go to the club." Their relationship was rapidly changing as Madonna was attaining full celebrity status. More on that subject later. . . .

Madonna: Darling of the Media

The last three months of 1984 witnessed the beginning of the full-fledged media explosion that centered around Madonna. In America, in the rock music business, you know that you've really arrived when your picture is on the cover of *Rolling Stone* magazine. You are a recognized media sensation in Middle America when that happens to you, and for Madonna it was the November 22, 1984, issue. The cover story was titled: "Madonna Goes All The Way," and with "Like A Virgin," indeed she had. The legend on the index page of the magazine summed up the thrust of the article by proclaiming: "How a sexy Motor City dancer went belly up with ballet and crossed the borderline into rock stardom—with a little help from her boyfriends." The tone of the article is a bit cynical, but the cover story signified that Madonna was a "main stream" hit, and that's all that mattered.

While we're on the subject of *Rolling Stone*, in both the January 17 and January 31, 1985, issues of the bi-weekly magazine, Madonna's *Like A Virgin* was the number-one album, number-one U.S. single, and number-one dance track.

Madonna has become the ultimate crossover artist in the music world, and now she is pulling the same stunt in the fashion world. The November 1984 issue of the respected high-fashion Bible, *Harper's Bazaar*, featured a four-page full-color spread on Madonna, deliciously photographed by the man who helped make portrait photography an art: Francesco Scavullo. Yes, in one shot she does show us that yummy tummy of hers, but the emphasis is on the perfect bone structure in her face. She looks outrageously hot in a totally classy high-fashion context.

In the little bio that accompanies the fashion spread, Madonna is quoted as saying, "The very best thing about single life is there's always someone else. And, besides, I wouldn't wish being Mr. Madonna on anybody."

Madonna Gets Physical

According to Madonna, "I swim one hundred laps every day to keep in shape. It's good to have a supple body; you can move around easily and it's a lot more visually appealing. You feel better too when you're at a normal weight."

Well, apparently Madonna's on-screen diet of Cheese Doodles while filming *Desperately Seeking Susan* got a bit out of control, because in December 1984 Madonna registered herself at Rancho La Puerta health spa near Tijuana, Mexico, to shape up a bit. Fresh from the ritzy "fat farm," Madonna slimmed down a touch for a sleek entry into her biggest year yet—1985!

11

"Material Girl"

THE WEEK AFTER FOREIGNER'S "I Want To Know Where Love Is" knocked Madonna's "Like A Virgin" off the top of the singles chart in *Billboard* magazine's "Hot 100," the single "Material Girl" was released as both a twelve-inch disco single, and as a seven-inch 45 rpm single. "Like A Virgin" had been the number-one song in America for a solid six weeks, and Madonna was preparing to do it all over again with "Material Girl"!

January 1985 found Madonna all over the radio airwaves, and on the television screen as well. In the beginning of the month, it was announced that Madonna was among the nominees for the American Music Awards, to be presented in a three-hour television special, broadcast live on January 28. Madonna's nomination was in the category of Favorite Female Pop Vocalist, and she was up against Cyndi Lauper and

Linda Ronstadt. On the awards telecast, Madonna made a brief appearance with Huey Lewis, presenting the award for Favorite Black Album/Male to Prince and the Revolution for *Purple Rain*.

When it came time for the category that Madonna was nominated in, Cyndi Lauper won. But, like the Grammy Award nominations that also came out in January 1985, these awards did not encompass the *Like A Virgin* album or single, nor the ''Material Girl'' single. The cut-off point for the annual Grammy Awards is October 15, so we can look forward to Madonna taking trophies in 1986—she could even be up for an Oscar!

On ''The American Music Awards'' Madonna was pressed in a black corset, and on her head she had an outlandish blond fall that cascaded down the right side of her head. Naturally, she was swathed in a multitude of crucifixes and black rubber bracelets.

The ''Material Girl'' Video

The video for the song ''Material Girl'' is outrageous and shows a totally different facet of multitalented Madonna. The video was shot at the Renmar Studios in Hollywood in the beginning of January 1985. It was produced by Simon Fields for Limelight Productions, directed by Mary Lambert, with Peter Sinclair as the cinematographer. Originally, Madonna had chosen Jean-Paul Goude to direct the video, but when she didn't like his ideas, she hired Mary Lambert to direct the video in compliance with Madonna's vision of what the concept should be.

The video opens with a shot of the backs of the heads of two cinematographers in a Hollywood screening room. On the viewing screen before them, we see a clapper board for "Maddona/Scene 3B/Take 5," filming on January 10, 1985. Silently, we see Madonna's close-up full screen in front of them.

Cut to Keith Carradine as the bearded big-time film director viewing Madonna's reel. "She's a star!" he insists. "How do I meet her?" he snaps at the studio flunky seated next to him.

Cut to the elaborate staircase set that Madonna has just finished filming her big scene on. We see a young director hand Madonna a boxed gift.

Cut to Madonna's dressing room and a diamond necklace in a black-velvet-lined box. Madonna is dishing the dirt on the phone with one of her girlfriends, telling her how expensive gifts can't buy her affections. Carradine overhears the conversation and realizes that he has to take another tack.

Cut to the production number of a lifetime! It's Madonna doing "Material Girl" with the same dress, hairdo, and much of the same choreography that Marilyn Monroe used when she sang "Diamonds Are A Girl's Best Friend" in the 1953 Howard Hawks movie *Gentlemen Prefer Blondes*. Madonna is gorgeous in her 1950s pink satin, ankle-length, shoulderless gown and three-quarter-length evening gloves. Over the gloves she wears sparkling diamond bracelets, from her ears dangle diamond earrings, and from around her neck dangles an elaborate diamond necklace.

The video is a classic, and has to be credited in part for making "Material Girl" another number-one hit. In the lavish production number, Madonna is lifted and slung about by a league of handsome men in black tuxedo tailcoats, while our favorite diva croons how she's just a "material girl"! Along the way, midnumber she picks her suitors' pockets and ends up with a downpour of cash, an ermine wrap, and everyone's hearts—naturally! I love it!

In the end Carradine wins Madonna's hand (etc.) with a bouquet of daisies. Hmmmm. Which is the real Madonna—the gold-digging chorus girl or the down-to-earth actress? You decide.

The video clip for "Material Girl" debuted on MTV February 1, 1985. When the single "Material Girl" debuted on the *Billboard* singles chart the week of February 9, 1985, it entered at number forty-three, two positions higher than Mick Jagger's first-ever solo single, "Just Another Night." Madonna was even giving Mick some stiff competition!

The promotional copy of the twelve-inch Jellybean remix of "Material Girl" is another clever merchandising tool, as it was shipped in a special scented sleeve! Madonna-mania was well under way and sweeping the globe.

Vision Quest

February also saw an additional Madonna single and two more videos! At long last the movie, the soundtrack, and the theme song from the Jon Peters production of *Vision Quest* was released. Madonna appeared in the movie, appeared in two promotional videos, and sang the first hit singles culled from the album!

Both songs were produced for the soundtrack album

by John "Jellybean" Benitez, and they were released as a two-sided single, giving Madonna three singles on the charts at once!

The rock number "Gambler" was written by Madonna. Unlike any of the cuts on her albums, "Gambler" is straight rock and roll, with a danceable beat. The ballad is titled "Crazy For You," and again represents a departure from the Madonna sound we're used to. It's a beautiful song composed by John Bettis and John Lind. "Crazy For You" is a great showcase for Madonna as a serious singer, and for Jellybean as a producer of much more scope than he's ever been given credit for. Timewise these two songs were produced between the *Madonna* and *Like A Virgin* LPs.

In both of the promotional videos, we see footage of Madonna performing the songs with a rock band backing her, and interspersed with scenes from the action of the movie.

"We shot it in Spokane, Washington. It was very cold, lonely, and boring," recalls Madonna. "Jon [Peters] and I met for another movie that he's producing, and when it came time for *Vision Quest*, they didn't want to get someone they had to direct; they didn't want to get an actress to pretend she's a singer. They wanted someone with a lot of style already." Well, they obviously chose the right girl!

As a film, *Vision Quest* is like a combination of *Rocky* and *Footloose* set in a high school wrestling team. The soundtrack is as dynamically important as the plot of the film. Shot on location in Spokane, Washington *Vision Quest* stars Matthew Modine as a determined wrestler who keeps dropping his weight so he can be the number-one contender in a tougher weight classification. Along the way, he falls in love with Linda Fiorentino and grapples with his own identity.

Madonna's one scene is set onstage at a club where Modine goes to rock-and-roll. The song "Gambler," which Madonna composed and sings, lasts in the film about thirty seconds. The ballad she sings, "Crazy For You," gets five-second flashes of her onstage, and is used as a recurring theme. Madonna's performance is brief and is billed as a "Special Appearance." Indeed, it is more fleeting than her appearances in the promotional videos that went into "heavy rotation" on MTV.

The film was actually more entertaining than I expected. Matthew Modine is quite good, and Madonna was fun to see, brief as her appearance was. Oddly, the versions of the two songs used in the movie were produced by Phil Ramone and Jellybean, but Jellybean does not get screen credit. On the "Original Soundtrack Album," new versions of the songs were recorded, and produced by John "Jellybean" Benitez alone. Between the time the movie was shot and released, Madonna had become a huge recording star, so they wanted stronger performances for the *Vision Quest* LP than were originally done by Ramone and Benitez.

More Madonna Hits

At this same time, Madonna was also on the charts as a video star and as a songwriter. Her debut "Madonna" video cassette (Warner Music Video) was in the nation's top twenty, and "Sidewalk Talk," the song that Madonna wrote for Jellybean's *Wotupski*!?! album, became the number-one song on the dance charts.

12

Jellybean
on Madonna

As I was assembling this book, the Madonna legend was growing by leaps and bounds on a day-to-day basis. Many publications were portraying her as a manipulating dominatrix who used men ruthlessly to better her career. When mention of Madonna's boyfriend of the past two years came up, no one was quite certain how to portray his role in her life. One of my sources announced to me that she knew that Madonna was dating a prominent Los Angeles lawyer who wanted to get into the record business, and the *New York Post* suddenly announced that Madonna was having a fling with actor Sean Penn, whom she had been seeing in Los Angeles and New York.

It was the same week that all sorts of rumors were flying about the loves of Madonna that I again interviewed Jellybean. It was a cold and snowy New York night in February 1985. We met at the Greenwich Village restaurant Gotham to discuss all the aspects of his professional *and* romantic relationship with our favorite "material girl."

John "Jellybean" Benitez was concerned that I get all my facts straight, both for this book and for all the magazine writing I was doing about Madonna. We candidly talked about Madonna's goals, glories, and aspirations. Our conversation was filled with all sorts of controversial information that had never previously been discussed about Madonna the musician and the movie star.

MARK: Tell me about the spring 1985 Madonna
         concert tour.
JOHN: Probably April will be the beginning of it,
         March or April. It's supposed to last a few
         weeks. It's just a U.S. tour.
MARK: Has she picked a band out yet?
JOHN: She's using the guys that toured as the
         Jacksons' band.
MARK: So Jonathan Moffit . . .
JOHN: I know: Pat Leonard, he's the keyboard
         player, and a guy named "Sugarfoot" is
         the drummer.
MARK: Yeah, Jonathan "Sugarfoot" Moffit.
JOHN: So those guys will be part of it.
MARK: I see where they're going to release the single
         "Crazy For You" from the *Vision Quest*
         soundtrack album. Is that going to compete
         with "Material Girl" on the charts?
JOHN: Yes. They're putting out a seven-inch right
         now. The A side is "Crazy For You." It's
         the love theme from *Vision Quest*. On the

LP is "Gambler," and they're both songs that I produced for Madonna. It's coming out on Geffen Records, not Sire.

MARK: The videos for those two songs, which are on MTV now, are basically from footage from the film, aren't they?

JOHN: Yes, but she's in the videos more than she is in the actual film.

MARK: So they had a lot of excess footage of her?

JOHN: When you see the videos, you think that she's in the film singing the whole song, both songs actually, but they don't use her in the movie that much. They just cut back to her for a line and then cut to the people in the movie.

MARK: Let's go back to 1982. You described an episode to me when "Everybody" came out and she was promoting it in the clubs.

JOHN: That would be October or November of 1982. She came to The Fun House with Bobby Shaw, and they were taking her around to the clubs to meet all the influential DJs and get her record played.

MARK: You said that you both gave each other the cold shoulder.

JOHN: We were, like, playing with each other. We were attracted to each other, but we were just playing with each other. I was immediately attracted to her. We exchanged numbers and started talking to each other on the phone. I was going back and forth to L.A., so I would call from L.A. We kept trying to set up to meet, then make a plan and end up canceling it because I had to be in the studio and she had to go to Europe, or something. We had a big scheduling problem. She had just finished some songs on her album, and they were putting out the next twelve-inch, and they wanted me to mix it, so I went to dinner with her and Michael Rosenblatt, the A&R [artist and repertoire] guy at Sire who signed her, and Bobby Shaw, at Shun Lee in the East Fifties. That's where they asked me to mix "Physical Attraction."

MARK: That was the twelve-inch of "Physical Attraction" and "Burning Up," and you mixed both of those?

JOHN: Well, not the twelve-inch version of "Burning Up." The album was completed, and they asked me to remix "Lucky Star" and "Burning Up." What they were actually asking me to do was go in and do all this production on it.

MARK: Create new bridges and musical passages?

JOHN: No, do guitar parts and new vocals, percussion, lay some tracks. It's the first time I ever did that when I was mixing a record.

MARK: Was this, for you, really your beginning in producing?

JOHN: I had already done "Flashdance."

MARK: You had remixed that?

JOHN: Yes, and I was just starting to mix a lot of major artists because of that.

MARK: I remember going into the studio one night

around midnight, and you were working on "Flashdance."

JOHN: I really had a lot of success as a mixer, and people kept telling me, "You're more of a producer." So, what I was doing was additional production, or co-producing. But I didn't have that much power to say, "I want co-production credit." I was just doing it because I want the record to sound good. So I went in and did all these new guitar parts on "Lucky Star." The guitars you hear on "Burning Up" and "Lucky Star" on the album are all new parts that Reggie Lucas didn't do. And there's new vocal parts. Even though those songs were produced by him, those weren't only produced by him, because I went in and did all this additional production on it— and totally different mixes. Then there was this other song called "Ain't No Big Deal."

MARK: Which ended up on the album *Revenge Of The Killer B's, Volume 2*.

JOHN: Right. It's written by Steve Bray, and he didn't want Madonna to use it on her album. So they had a slot for another song.

MARK: So it was a problem with him as the songwriter; it wasn't that they didn't like the song?

JOHN: From what I understood, "Ain't No Big Deal" is the song that Madonna got signed for—that's what they were signing her to do. And Mark [Kamins] had come in and

done it, and they didn't like it that much. So
they had him go in and do "Everybody."
And they put "Ain't No Big Deal" on the
shelf. Then they gave the album to Reggie
Lucas and said, "We might as well put
'Ain't No Big Deal' on the album." So then
Reggie did a version, and Warner Brothers
originally wanted me to mix overdubs on
"Lucky Star," "Burning Up," and "Ain't
No Big Deal." So that's when I first met
Steve Bray. But then we were gonna work
on not Reggie Lucas' version, not Mark
Kamins' version, but the version that Steve
Bray and Madonna did together as a demo
originally. So I was going to do all of these
overdubs on that. But then, Steve Bray sold
the song to an artist called Baracuda on Epic
Records, and they put out the song, and
they didn't want two versions of the same
song coming out at once, so he said they
[Baracuda] could have it. So at that point
Madonna's album was finished, "Burning
Up" and "Physical Attraction" were
moving up the dance chart, and they had no
album to come out. And they're rushing to
get this album out, and Madonna's like:
"Oh, shit, I need a new song now, because
I don't have a song." In comes "Holiday."

MARK: So this is May 1983?
JOHN: Late April, early May. I had the song
          "Holiday," I got it from Curtis Hudson
          and Lisa Stevens from this group called
          Pure Energy.

MARK: You offered the song to Mary Wilson, and
        you said you offered it to someone else.
        Who was that?

JOHN: I offered it to the A&R guy at Arista
        Records for Phyllis Hyman. He thought it
        was okay, but it didn't blow his mind. After
        Mary rejected it and Phyllis Hyman
        rejected it, my gut feeling was that this is a
        hit, and someone is going to do it. When
        Madonna heard it, she liked it right away.
        She didn't have much choice; she had to get
        her album done. This was the first time I
        had ever produced a record by myself. So
        everything that I was doing was new to me,
        and I was trying to plan everything and get
        everything together and come in under
        budget and make everyone happy and try to
        do the best job I could possibly do. And I
        was really excited that I was going to
        produce my first record. It was, like, the
        next step.

MARK: So "Holiday" was your first shot at being a
        full-fledged producer?

JOHN: Yes, and I wanted it more than anything. I
        had worked so hard DJing, I was not letting
        this go by. It came out really good. I went
        in and did the whole thing in three or four
        days. I was, like, sleeping in the studio, and
        I didn't know how I was going to get
        through it. I think it was, like, a desire on
        my part to really accomplish something.

MARK: I know that you've mentioned a couple of
        times that you would test records on a dance

floor when you're working with a mix on them, just to see what the crowd reaction is. Did you do this with "Holiday"?

JOHN: Oh, yes. I went to The Fun House during the day and put it on their system and listened to how it would sound on the dance floor. Then, when that was done and the *Madonna* album came out, "Lucky Star" was supposed to be the first single, and no one liked "Holiday": "Yeah, it's okay, but 'Lucky Star' is the smash." In the back of my mind, I'm going, "Well, I don't know. I think 'Holiday' is a hit." So they put out a twelve-inch promo on "Holiday" and "Lucky Star." "Lucky Star" was the A side, and "Holiday" was the B side [DJ edition only]. I knew as soon as DJs saw "John 'Jellybean' Benitez" on the "Holiday" side, that was it, because DJs stick together. It worked really well, because "Holiday" became a number-one dance record. At the time Madonna had just gotten a manager. When I first met Madonna, she didn't have a lawyer or a manager or an accountant or a bank account. So she had this manager, Freddy DeMann, and he worked the record company into working the record.

MARK: So Freddy was on the case when "Holiday" came out?

JOHN: Yes, and then it went . . . It became a pop record. It didn't have a video, and went to number sixteen on the pop chart. Had there been a video, it probably would have been much bigger.

MARK: After that they brought out the special twelve-inch of "Lucky Star"/ "Borderline"?

JOHN: Yes. Well, what happened was they said, "Okay, we need the next single while we start the next album [*Like A Virgin*] so we can have something in between, so they gave me "Borderline." And when I first heard it, I was, like, "No one is ever going to dance to this record!" I thought it was a great pop song and a great radio record, but I never thought it was ever going to be a dance record. So they asked me to go in, and what I did was the same thing that I did to "Burning Up" and "Lucky Star." So this time I said, "If you want me to go in [and] just mix this the way it is and just give me mix credit, I can't do it. Because if I mix this record, it's just going to sound like a better version than what's there now. If you want me to go in and do overdubs and everything, you're gonna have to give me co-production credit."

So they said, "All right, if you go in and do it, and we like it, we'll give you co-production credit. If we don't, we'll just put out the version that we have."

MARK: So on that twelve-inch there are still the pieces that Reggie Lucas originally put down, plus your additional rerecorded segments?

JOHN: Right. So, what I did was I added an all-
        new bass guitar to it; there's new
        synthesizers on it, there's new background
        vocal parts, there's percussion added to it.
        So what happened was, I was just going to
        do it as a dance record, then they liked it so
        much, they had me edit it down to a seven-
        inch [45-rpm single] version. But
        "Borderline" is not a hit in England. They
        wanted to go with "Lucky Star." So I said,
        okay. So when I did a twelve-inch of
        "Lucky Star" from the album, I thought
        that I could have done a more outrageous
        dance version. This was my chance to make
        "Lucky Star" more danceable, so I made
        it, and they made a video to my version for
        Europe, and it was a big hit in Europe.
        Then "Borderline" was a big hit in
        America, so they decided, "Well, let's just
        give the video to MTV." Then the video
        got on MTV and just exploded! And they
        hadn't released a single of "Lucky Star"
        over here yet, so they did. Maybe they had
        this all planned, and they never told
        Madonna, but when she found out that
        "Lucky Star" was coming out as a single,
        she was really not happy.

MARK: Because she was not happy with that song?

JOHN: Because the whole *Like A Virgin* album was
        done already and ready to go.

MARK: Oh, I see, so it was in the can last summer!

JOHN: Yes, they were ready to go with *Like A
        Virgin*, and they said, "Oh, no, wait,

radio's playing 'Lucky Star,' and MTV's on it; we're just gonna go with 'Lucky Star.' " So then when "Lucky Star" sold a million and a half records for the album, she already had the ball rolling.

MARK: So the way was already paved for *Like A Virgin*?

JOHN: Yes, they were ready to release *Like A Virgin* until MTV started playing the "Lucky Star" video. And then all of these radio stations got requests for "Lucky Star." So the *Madonna* album had already had "Everybody" as a single, "Physical Attraction" and "Burning Up," then "Holiday," then "Borderline," "Lucky Star," so she was sitting on that album for a year and a half! The *Like A Virgin* album could have come out right after "Borderline."

MARK: So, when did she record the *Like A Virgin* album?

JOHN: In April of 1984.

MARK: Now, when she went into the studio to record *Like A Virgin*, had you already produced Madonna's "Gambler" and "Crazy For You" for the *Vision Quest* soundtrack?

JOHN: Phil Ramone and I did it for the soundtract in November of 1983. We did it in Los Angeles. The movie took a long time—it was supposed to come out in March 1984. It didn't come out until February 1985. By then Madonna was a big star. And they didn't like the way the movie versions came out, so they had me go in and redo "Gambler" and "Crazy For You."

MARK: So the versions that you and Phil Ramone did aren't on the album?

JOHN: Right, but in the movie the versions that Phil Ramone and I did together are used.

MARK: Let's talk about your personal relationship with Madonna. You started dating in the fall of 1982?

JOHN: Yes, but it wasn't really a monogamous relationship until the spring of 1983—up until recently. We had gone through changes just like any other couple. We'd break up for a week or two.

MARK: When did she get her loft in SoHo?

JOHN: In August of 1983. She went from Fourth Street, to Thirteenth Street, to SoHo. We were living together in SoHo until we started not getting along now. That's all about the personal stuff! [He laughs.]

MARK: I'll let you get away with that [laughing]. You mentioned to me earlier that things started changing. That you couldn't go to restaurants unless the lighting was dark enough or everyone would recognize Madonna and mob the table. When did things start to change?

JOHN: Right after the "Borderline" video, people started noticing her a lot. I mean, people used to notice her a lot just from walking down the street.

MARK: You mean, just from the way she would be dressed?

JOHN: Right. And then people would bother her. I really shouldn't say "bother" her, but fans would come over all the time and want autographs and stuff. So it was a learning experience for her, something she had to adjust to.

MARK: She was kind of new to it too. Did she take to it, or was she put off by it?

JOHN: I've seen her sometimes put people off, but with good reason. Recently, when we were coming back from our Christmas vacation in St. Martin, on the plane she didn't want to give any autographs at all; she was on vacation! And I had to agree with her. It was, like, constantly, constantly people hounding her: "Madonna! Madonna! Madonna!" She has, like, little kids and young girls, and sometimes it's difficult if you're not really in the mood.

MARK: Yeah, to be "on" every minute.

JOHN: So she was in one of those moods. It was a really difficult plane flight, because people kept wanting to take pictures, and everybody's on vacation, so they wanted her autograph, so I was like a security guard the whole way back. These little girls kept coming over and trying to take a picture, and I kept blocking Madonna's face with a magazine. And this woman comes over and says she wanted an autograph and it was the least that Madonna could do, because she

was a pediatrician, and she works very hard
for her kids to buy Madonna records. It was
like half of the plane was rooting for
Madonna, and half of the plane was rooting
for the other woman. And then coming
back through customs, by then word had
spread through the whole plane that
Madonna was on the plane. But I find that it
really depends on the type of people. Let's
say someone like Barbra Streisand has,
like, an older audience, and I'm sure that if
someone over twenty-one saw Barbra
Streisand and wanted an autograph, they
wouldn't run over screaming, "BARBRA
STREISAND!" Whereas, little kids go,
"MADONNA!"

MARK: Because that's her audience.

JOHN: Right. She appeals to a very youthful
audience. I think that she has a lot of
responsibility to herself, and to them.
Sometimes you have to draw the line. So I
can see not wanting to be bothered all of the
time.

MARK: You want to be recognized and appreciated
on one hand, but then again you want to be
able to go to the grocery store and not be
harassed.

JOHN: She's strong personally, and she'll grow
used to it.

MARK: In a way it has all happened to Madonna
very quickly, hasn't it?

JOHN: Well, in my eyes, I always thought she was
a superstar, the moment she walked into the

DJ booth. Because I've seen so many artists coming over, trekking in with their record, and there was just something about Madonna. I said, "This girl's gonna be a star!" Not just like *any* star; she was definitely gonna be big. This was a long time before anyone else saw that, way ahead of radio stations.

MARK: Your career has obviously changed because of your work on Madonna's "Holiday." Can you trace it to that?

JOHN: It would have been something else that I produced if it hadn't been that. It just happened that that song was a hit. Regardless of who sang it, I think it would have been a hit. I'm sure that Madonna's performance on it helped a lot. The timing was perfect.

MARK: When Madonna decided to go with Nile Rodgers for the *Like A Virgin* album, I understand that Reggie Lucas was sort of put off that he didn't get a shot at the second album. What was the story?

JOHN: Well, I ended up remixing everything that Reggie did! I wasn't surprised. I mean, Reggie's good, but I think she made the right decision. She spoke to about twenty producers.

MARK: Were you ever under consideration for the *Like A Virgin* album?

JOHN: To do, like, one or two songs. It was a mutual decision that because of the relationship, it wouldn't be a good thing to do. And I didn't want people to think that the only reason that I was producing Madonna was that I was her boyfriend. I wanted people to think that what I did was good, and I think that if I would have done it, it would have been more detrimental to me later down the road. I helped her find producers. She read me a list of people, and then I have a vast record collection, so I gave her what I thought represented a wide variety of music of different producers' work. And Nile's good.

MARK: Did she consult you on the final decision?

JOHN: Every night before we went to sleep; "Well, what do you think? I'm not sure." I don't want to mention who else she was considering, but I was just, "Go with what you feel is best. You've always done that, and it's always helped you. Trust your instincts. Go with what you feel is right."

MARK: So the decision was really up to her? It wasn't up to Freddy DeMann at all?

JOHN: No. Madonna makes all her own decisions. No one tells her what to do. She has other people carry out different things for her that might be awkward for her as an artist to do, but Madonna basically is Madonna.

MARK: In control of her own fate?

JOHN: Right. She knows what she wants, and she goes after it. That's one of the qualities that I admire the most about her, because I always was the type of person that, when I wanted something, I went after it.

MARK: So it was an aspect that both you and
            Madonna could mutually identify with?

JOHN: Right. Up until then I always had trouble
            with girls—when you spend so much time
            DJing and always working in the studio.
            Madonna always understood all of those
            things. It worked for me, and it worked for
            her too, because she always had boyfriends
            who could never quite understand what she
            wanted to be, what she wanted to do, or
            how much work it took to get what she
            wanted to be. And me, having a basic
            understanding of the music business, I
            understood that she wanted to be an artist,
            and there are certain things that you have to
            do to get there.

MARK: This brings me to a rather sharp-edged
            question. A lot of writers are writing about
            Madonna having gotten to where she is
            through the men she's dated. On the other
            hand, all of these guys seem like they're
            still charmed by her, even though they
            claim they've been used by her. Let's face
            it, all of us in the business use each other to
            a certain extent.

JOHN: Madonna just makes it more obvious, and
            there's nothing wrong with that. I never
            felt, when they did stories on her and they
            always talked about all the boyfriends she
            used—like the boyfriend who taught her
            how to play [Dan Gilroy], and Steve Bray
            helped her with her demo, and Mark
            Kamins got her signed—and then they get to

the point where I'm at, and I just don't fit into the story anymore. It was, like, "Well, not yet, but he's coming—he's next." But I never quite fit into "one of the boyfriends that was used." I never thought that. To a degree, we helped each other out a lot. We could look at it and say, "Wow, I really used her. I ended up producing a song on her album." But I don't think that we used each other; I think that we really helped each other a lot. I think that helping relationships last longer today because we're both very ambitious.

MARK: In a way, both of your careers began moving upward at the same pace.

JOHN: Had I never mixed any Madonna records, I would have become just as successful as I am right now, because I've had so many other number-one hits without Madonna. I've had [mixing assignments on] sixteen or seventeen number-one records, two of which were Madonna's. And when you ask me about the production end of things, a lot of people know that I did "Holiday," but a lot of people aren't hiring me to produce records because of "Holiday."

MARK: Although you didn't produce *Like A Virgin*, being brought in to remix what Nile had done, how did you feel—especially after having produced "Holiday"?

JOHN: I wasn't going to do it at first. I passed on it. I thought, "I've produced a number-ten record, and a number-sixteen record. It

would be a step backwards now to go and
mix something. But I just felt it didn't really
matter. Nile went in and did something, and
it was good, but he did something for the
twelve-inch, but Warner Brothers wanted a
different perspective. So I went in and did
some overdubs that I thought would make it
more danceable. And then they went with
my version. What I did worked. If you
listen to the album version or the seven-
inch, and the twelve-inch, there's a
noticeable difference. There's different
instruments. I added a lot of stuff that
makes it work better: the cowbell, the
synthesizer that has the "chimney" bell
part. At first I thought it was a bad idea, but
my lawyer and Madonna's lawyer said,
"Hey, would you do it?" and the manager
called me, the head of A&R at Warner
Brothers called me, Madonna asked me. So
I just figured, "Well, why not? I mix
everybody else's records." I did some
things to make it a number-one dance
record, and it was.

MARK: It happened very quickly, didn't it?

JOHN: It was the fastest number-one record ever
on the dance charts.

MARK: How long was that?

JOHN: Four weeks to number one! I just did
[remixed] "Material Girl" now, and I did a
twelve-inch of "Dress You Up." "Dress
You Up" is supposed to be released in
England, but I don't know what the status

is. It will probably follow "Material Girl."
"Dress You Up" is tremendous. It's a
number-one dance record. It's really
different. I added all this percussion stuff
and drum machines and stuff, so it moves
really well. Steve Bray programmed all the
percussion and drum stuff on it.

MARK: So he's real active?

JOHN: He and I worked together on a lot of stuff.
He arranged and played some of the parts
on "Sidewalk Talk" on my album, which
Madonna wrote.

MARK: Which went to number one on the dance
charts. You and Madonna were both just in
California for the American Music Awards.
Did you both go out there just for that show?

JOHN: I was remixing Barbra Streisand's
"Emotion," a song for Kenny Loggins,
and two new Donna Summer records.
Madonna went out there to do the
"Material Girl" video, then she went to
Hawaii, then to Japan, then back to L.A.,
then we went to the American Music
Awards together.

MARK: And in Hawaii she did the photo sessions
for her 1986 calendar?

JOHN: Right. She did her calendar in Hawaii and
went to Japan to promote the Like A Virgin
album. Then we went to the awards, and I
came back to New York.

MARK: Since Like A Virgin was recorded so far in
advance of its release, is she already
planning album number three?

JOHN: I don't think so. They have so many singles
        to pick from, then the tour, the two movies,
        and then this book. [He laughs.]

MARK: She's gonna be all over the place!

JOHN: Madonna's very unpredictable. I know that
        Madonna's very much into doing films. I
        think [she'll] do at least another film in the
        next year.

MARK: I sat up last night watching Marilyn Monroe
        doing ''Diamonds Are A Girl's Best
        Friend'' from *Gentlemen Prefer Blondes*,
        and then put on Madonna's ''Material
        Girl'' video. It's amazing how the musical
        number is almost identical—the same dress,
        the same choreography, everything!

JOHN: That was all Madonna's idea. They had
        come up with another concept, and she's,
        like, ''No, I think this is the way to go:
        'Diamonds Are A Girl's Best Friend'!'' She
        really said, ''No, this is what I want!''
        She's, like, really in control of what she
        wants.

MARK: Now, did Jean-Paul Goude work on that? I
        know that he was originally supposed to.

JOHN: He came up with another concept, which
        they didn't use. Then Mary Lambert came
        up with another concept and Madonna said,
        ''No, no, I want to do this, and I think that
        it's very commercial for the MTV
        viewers.'' It's perfect!

MARK: How do you feel about everyone drawing
        correlations between Madonna and Marilyn
        Monroe?

JOHN: People are always trying to make
          comparisons—calling Sean Penn the new
          Robert De Niro. I think that Madonna is
          just Madonna. I can definitely see Madonna
          living out certain Marilyn Monroe kind of
          traits, and she is definitely a BIG Marilyn
          fan! I think she's more like Carole Lombard
          than Marilyn. When I see Carole Lombard
          films, she's more like that. Madonna isn't
          going to be like anyone else—she's
          Madonna. I think that Madonna is going to
          be an even bigger actress than she is a singer.

MARK: Do you think that your relationship with
          Madonna will last?

JOHN: I think that the relationship will run its
          course, just like any other relationship. If it
          was meant to be, it will last. I'm a real
          strong believer in fate. I think that it was
          really good that we ended up meeting when
          we met, because we helped each other
          through some very difficult times, going
          through the last two years of our lives. The
          timing was right when we met. We were
          both, like, *there*. We just had to make the
          right moves to get to the next step—and we
          both did—and helping each other along the
          way really had a lot to do with it. We were
          there for each other when we needed each
          other. If both of us keep working at the
          same pace, it will continue.

          I was always the type of guy that I didn't
          want to have any girl in the way or anything
          that was gonna stop me. And Madonna is

the same way. So if our goals change and
we can't really be together anymore, I
didn't want to really dwell on if it's gonna
last. Our work demands so much of us, then
when we come home, there's not very
much left to give. But that makes both of us
happy. Madonna was able to understand
that about me, and I was able to understand
that about her. I think that we'll always be
friends, and we'll always be supportive.
We were friends before we were lovers, and
I think that's an important part of our
relationship.

Like I said, she always makes her own
decisions, and I could just sit there and
listen and give her my advice, but
ultimately she would make her own
decisions. It was an ideal situation for the
time period, up until right now. Where it
goes tomorrow—who knows? I can't really
say. It was a good relationship, and it was
fulfilling, and I'm sure that she feels the
same way, regardless of what happens.

George Bernard Shaw has a quote:
"People that get ahead in this world are the
people that look for the circumstances they
want, and when they don't find them, they
make them!"

That quote obviously applies to both Madonna and
Jellybean. They helped each other with their respec-
tive careers, and who knows what the future holds for
them as a couple? But as individuals they are both

going to do exactly what is necessary for both of their own visions of self-fulfillment. My conversation with Jellybean really focused many of my observations on Madonna, and in many ways he was more direct in his observations about Madonna than she was in talking to me about herself.

This interview filled me in on many facts and observations that were previously sketchy, assumed, or misquoted by other writers. After talking with Jellybean that night, I realized even further that Madonna isn't just the singing sensation of the season—she's a major superstar in the making, and for her this is just the beginning.

13
Madonna on Madonna

SHE'S THE MOODY CATHOLIC GIRL, the street-wise bad girl, the bratty coquette, the flirtatious rock singer, the vulnerable actress, and the self-confident child/ woman. She's a sexy Scavullo model, a *Harper's Bazaar* fashion plate, the spoiled kid in a wedding dress and a pair of spiked heels; she's the vamp in lingerie and cheap rubber bracelets, and the tomboy with rags tied in her hair and an athletic T-shirt cut off at her lowest rib. That's Madonna!

Some aspects of Madonna only she can explain, and here's her forum. La Madonna talks about Ms. Ciccone, the "Lucky Star" discusses the "Material Girl."

What does she think about herself? "I always wanted to be taller," she confesses. "I feel like a shrimp, but that's the way it goes. I'm five feet four inches—that's actually average. Everything about me is average; everything's normal, in the books. It's the things inside that make me not average. In my business career I feel I make good decisions, but in my personal life I'm constantly creating havoc by changing my mind every five seconds.''

Since Madonna is her actual name, does she go by any nicknames? ''My father called my Nonny. I think that's how I said my name when I was little,'' she recalls. ''I gave myself a graffiti tag too: 'Boy Toy.' '' What exactly does ''Boy Toy'' mean? ''It's what I am when I write graffiti. I like nicknames. I think Jellybean's got the best one, though. The name of my publishing company is 'Webo Girl.' It's actually a direct translation. *'Webo'* means 'ball shaker' in Spanish. But it's the name of a dance, like the Smurf. It's the way everybody was dancing awhile ago, and I named my publishing company that because me and this girl Debbie and this girl Claudia were the only white girls that could webo at The Roxy. And Kano, the graffiti artist, painted on the back of our jackets one of his paintings, one of his pieces, and it said, 'Webo Gals.' ''

How did Madonna learn to dance? According to her, ''I really learned on my own. I watched television a lot, and I used to try to copy Shirley Temple when I was a little girl. I used to turn on the record player and dance in the basement by myself and give dance lessons to my girlfriends in my five-year-old manner. As I got older, I started giving lessons to boys too, and I remember the first guy I gave lessons to. The song was 'Honky Tonk Woman' by the Stones. It was really sexy, right?—like stomping and grinding. When I was about twelve, I decided I should try to get pro about this and started going to the schools where they teach jazz, tap, baton twirling, and gymnastics. It was just a place to send hyperactive girls, basically.''

Madonna claims that her favorite possession is "a picture of my mother when she was young, and she was riding on a horse and smiling and laughing. She didn't give it to me. My mother died when I was real young, and when I moved to New York, I stole it from my father.''

What does her father think of her fashion sense? Madonna recalls Thanksgiving 1983. "I came home with black pants, a black T-shirt, no jewlery at all, and my hair just sort of not combed—that's pretty conservative. No boots or spikes or anything, and my father spent most of the time looking at me, going, 'You always dress like that? Is that a costume?' ''

What was her first Manhattan apartment like? Says Madonna, "The first apartment I ever had all by myself was on Fourth Street and Avenue B, and it was my pride and joy, because it was the worst possible neighborhood I could ever live in." Times have changed, however, and now she lives in the arty area of town, SoHo. "I live in a loft in New York City. It's vast and empty, two thousand square feet with wooden floors and windows on all sides. There 、 no furniture, only my bed and a kitchen table with chairs, plus all this electronic stuff and graffiti paintings on the walls.''

Now that her life-style has changed, how does this affect her relationship with her friends from her struggling days? "It's fashionable to slum," she explains, "to live with five people in an apartment and to wear the same outfit every day, to never comb your hair, and to live on jellybeans—no pun intended. You know, half the people I hung out with from the downtown area have totally snubbed me. They think that I'm selling out and stuff. If I go back to clubs, they won't talk to me. Nasty little digs like, 'Little Madonna, now she's a big star and she can't talk to us.' That's why I don't feel a real unity with all those people, because half of them have totally ousted me anyway. They say, like, 'Oh, she never really hung out anyway, she's not really downtown.' "

What are some of the "Like A Virgin" girl's firsts? Her first rock concert: "David Bowie at Cobo Hall in Detroit. Oh, it was the most marvelous thing I'd ever done in my life. I was punished severely for going." Her first infatuation with a member of the opposite sex: "The first boy I ever loved was Ronny Howard in my fifth-grade class. He had real white-blond hair and sky-blue eyes. He was so beautiful I wrote his name all over my sneakers, and on the playground I used to take off the top part of my uniform and chase him around!"

What does Madonna think of England? "They have lots of good clothes shops!" she enthuses. "I always have a good time shopping there because fashion is so important to English people. I didn't have time to find any good restaurants, but I like the way the cars are on the other side!"

If there was to be a "Madonna" doll, what would she be like? According to the real item: "The doll whose hair you don't have to comb! And the only things she says are, 'Stop pulling my hair!' 'Leave me alone!' 'How much money do you make?' or, 'Come here, little boy!' " She laughs.

Who are her favorite actresses? "Marilyn Monroe, Carole Lombard, Jessica Lange, Susan Sarandon." What is it that attracts her to Marilyn? Says Madonna,

"Her innocence and her sexuality and her humor and her vulnerability."

If Madonna had a dream date, would it be with (a) Lionel Richie, (b) Rick Springfield, (c) Simon LeBon of Duran Duran, or (d) David Lee Roth of Van Halen? According to her, "I wouldn't go out with any of them, if you want to know the truth. If I had to choose, I'd go out with David Lee Roth, but I wouldn't dress up for him!"

Would she ever consider doing a duet with a male rock star? Says Madonna, "I'm considering doing a song with Billy Idol, if you can believe it. Maybe a soul cover. That would be good because we're both white and plastic and blond."

Since TV's hit night-time soap opera *Dynasty* has stars like Rock Hudson, Ali MacGraw, and Diahann Carroll floating in and out of the cast, if Madonna was on the show, what kind of character would she like to play? "I'd play the girl who made Alexis [Joan Collins] feel like a fool. I'd like to trip her up!"

What doesn't Madonna like? "When people smoke, especially in elevators and closed-in places. It's just so rude." She continues on the subject, "I hate it when people stand around and go, 'Hi, how are you?' I hate words that don't have any reason or meaning."

· Having come from a Catholic upbringing, how did Madonna feel about losing her virginity? Says she, "I thought of it as a career move!"

What is Madonna proficient at? According to her, "Manipulating people—that's what I'm good at!"

Well, that's what life in the fast lane has been like for Madonna. At the age of twenty-five, she's found that the glamorous life is here and now for her, and she's ready for more!

14

Vinyl Virgin
or Material Girl?

HOW DOES MADONNA VIEW her new-found fame? According to her, "I have more bills, my telephone rings more, I look down at the ground more when I'm walking. I take people out to dinner more, and sometimes I get this scary feeling that I could do anything I wanted." You know something? She's probably right!

Does she like being a celebrity? "It depends what kind of mood I'm in. Sometimes I want people to notice me, when I'm feeling like I really need to have my ego boosted and stuff, and sometimes I want everyone to leave me alone. I miss being anonymous. I miss being someone that people just looked at 'cause they thought I was interesting and not because they know who I am. If they know who you are, they think that they have the right to come up and ask you stuff, get things from you."

But on the other hand, Madonna has gained quite a lot lately: a movie career, two multimillion-selling international hit albums, and a big-time manager to boot! Whatever Madonna's wanted, she's gotten. She recalls how she became a client of Michael Jackson's former manager, Freddy DeMann. "This guy didn't know me from a hole in the wall. I wasn't going to say, 'Please, oh, please, manage me.' I said, 'If you're lucky, you're going to get to manage me because I'M going to take YOU places!' "

She's gained the respect of her co-workers in the entertainment business. Says Nile Rodgers, "Everyone told me she was a terrible ogre, but I thought she was great!" According to Michael Rosenblatt of Sire Records, "People expect her to be a dumb blonde, but she's not. She's got drive and she does her business." Movie director Susan Seidelman proclaims about Madonna, "It's an aura she has. I also think Madonna has an incredible face, almost like vintage movie stars like Garbo and Dietrich, a face you'd like to look at blown up to fifty feet high and thirty feet wide. She's more than a typical blond beauty!"

Madonna is stretching out in her career. Her portrayal of Susan in *Desperately Seeking Susan* has exposed another dimension of her talents and shown the world a bit more about herself. "Susan's a real adventurer; she's carefree, she's irresponsible—kind of like me," Madonna laughs. But does this signal the end of her recording career? "Hell, no!" snaps Madonna. "Movies are just another thing to do!"

She's made it perfectly clear that she's not afraid to take chances. "The important thing is not to be afraid," she says. "I think a lot of warnings that people give you about taking chances are usually their own inner voices saying, 'I'm afraid to do it, so you shouldn't do it either.' " That's obviously never been her problem. She adds, "I love making videos too, but I wish they were longer, and I wish I wasn't limited by the boundaries of the song. That's what's so much fun about films. They give you a chance to expand. That's what I want to do—always keep expanding!"

Thanks to the two cuts that she performed on the *Vision Quest* soundtrack, Madonna has shown two more sides of her vocal talents. However, she is quick to point out, "I'm proud of the fact that I started out as a rhythm-and-blues-oriented disco singer. It gave me more of an identity. I feel that the pop charts are finally opening to urban-contemporary sounds."

What about her love life? Will Madonna and Jellybean be together in the future? Says Jellybean, "We're working on a lot of things. I'm sure I'll still be mixing records for her. We'll be somewhat involved in each other's careers." I guess we'll just have to wait and see.

If Madonna were to have a new suitor come in to her life, what would he be like? According to her, "They'd have to be really funny and make me laugh all the time and give me lots of presents. They'd have to go out of the way to find things I was interested in and talk to me about them. And . . . they'd also have to TIE ME UP!"

Will she take to the success that has come upon her like a tidal wave lately? Easily. She's a real tough cookie who compares her attitude to that of Prince. "Sure I can relate to him, because he has a chip on his shoulder. He's competitive, from the Midwest, a screwed-up home, and he has something to prove. I can relate to all that—TOTALLY!"

One way or another, Madonna is out to make an impression on the world. Some people are enthralled, and some people are appalled, but one thing's for certain: they're all watching! In the book *The Rolling Stone Review 1985*, Madonna is listed in two categories for her industry profile during the calendar year 1984. She's one of eighteen of the year's "Female Sex Symbols," and she's one of five of the "Creeps of the Year." To them she's just the million-selling tart who's fun to snicker at, but you'd better believe that this "material girl" is having the last laugh—all the way to the bank!

However, she adds, "Success doesn't make you a better person. Hopefully the learning that you do and the education that you get as you are moving up makes you a better person, not the success. You know, it's nice to finally have a chance to do what you want to do—that's fulfilling. To say that you have the recognition and respect makes you feel good about yourself. It makes you feel like you've made the right decision, but I don't think that makes you a better person. A lot of times it will ruin you if you take it too seriously."

Madonna knows what she wants—more of everything! And she's not afraid to go out and get it. In a year that has already given her number-one records, a hit debut film, a Hollywood soundtrack album, a concert tour, and another solo album coming up, what else could Madonna want? How about a sexy calendar for 1986 with lots of hot exclusive photos? Or another movie in the works? Or a Grammy Award? Stay tuned; they're all coming up for Madonna. She's living proof that when you're a "material girl," and you play your cards right, you can turn your dreams into reality!

Who is Madonna? She represents so many different

things to different people. The interviews that I conducted to discover who she really is presented me with a multitude of vivid images: To Mark James Brooky she was just that cute high school cheerleader who was always doing something to get noticed. To Stephen Jon Lewicki she was the self-confident brunette who loved having the camera pointed at her. To Mark Kamins she was that flirting, special dancer looking for her opportunity to be discovered as a singer. To Jellybean she was that arrogant and alluring girl with the blond-streaked hair who was set on becoming famous. To Maripol she is the ultimate trend-setter who made crucifixes and black rubber bracelets into a fashion statement. To Susan Seidelman she is the New Wave Carole Lombard whose face begs to be blown up larger than life on the silver screen. To Reid Rosefelt she is the sharp-witted and highly professional young actress destined to make her mark in movies. And to me she is the determined yet vulnerable young star with an attitude, a strong sense of self, and a goal.

She's that aspiring young dancer from Pontiac, Michigan, in ripped leotards. She's the pushy counter girl at Dunkin' Donuts, set on making it big in Manhattan—at any cost. She's that white disco singer who lures everybody into celebrating with her. She's the bratty Catholic schoolgirl with rags tied in her hair. She's the tart in the wedding dress, rolling around on the stage floor of Radio City Music Hall and claiming that she feels "like a virgin." She's the gold-digging "material girl" who will stop at nothing to get what she wants!

To millions of record buyers, videophiles, and moviegoers around the world, she's the outlandish girl with the beauty mark and too much jewelry. She's aggressive, she's unique, she's sexy, she's gutsy, she's glamorous, and she's going to make sure that you remember her "look," her face, her voice, and her name. She's more than just a "lucky star." She's THE ultimate new multimedia superstar of the eighties —and her name is Madonna!

Madonna's Discography/ Videography/Filmography

ALBUMS:

Madonna (Sire Records 1-23867)
  Release date: July 1983

  Side One:
    "Lucky Star"
      Time: 5:30
      Writer: Madonna
      Producer: Reggie Lucas
      Engineer: Jim Dougherty
    "Borderline"
      Time: 5:18
      Writer: Reggie Lucas

Producer: Reggie Lucas
Engineer: Jim Dougherty
"Burning Up"
Time: 4:48
Writer: Madonna
Producer: Reggie Lucas
Engineer: Jim Dougherty
"I Know It"
Time: 3:45
Writer: Madonna
Producer: Reggie Lucas
Engineer: Jim Dougherty

Side Two:
"Holiday"
Time: 6:08
Writers: Curtis Hudson and Lisa Stevens
Producer: John "Jellybean" Benitez
Engineer: Michael Hutchinson
Mixing Engineer: Jay Mark
"Think Of Me"
Time: 4:53
Writer: Madonna
Producer: Reggie Lucas
Engineer: Jim Dougherty
"Physical Attraction"
Time: 6:35
Writer: Reggie Lucas
Producer: Reggie Lucas
Engineer: Jim Dougherty
"Everybody"
Time: 4:57
Writer: Madonna

Producer: Mark Kamins
Engineer: Butch Jones

Like A Virgin by Madonna (Sire Records 1-25157)
Release date: November 1984

Side One:
 "Material Girl"
 Time: 3:56
 Writers: Peter Brown and Robert Rans
 Producer: Nile Rodgers
 Engineers: Jason Corsaro, with Rob Eaton
 "Angel"
 Time: 3:53
 Writers: Madonna and Steve Bray
 Producer: Nile Rodgers
 Engineers: Jason Corsaro, with Rob Eaton
 "Like A Virgin"
 Time: 3:35
 Writers: Billy Steinberg and Tom Kelly
 Producer: Nile Rodgers
 Engineers: Jason Corsaro, with Rob Eaton
 "Over And Over"
 Time: 4:09
 Writers: Madonna and Steve Bray
 Producer: Nile Rodgers
 Engineers: Jason Corsaro, with Rob Eaton
 "Love Don't Live Here Anymore"
 Time: 4:45
 Writer: Miles Gregory
 Producer: Nile Rodgers
 Engineers: Jason Corsaro, with Rob Eaton

Side Two:
  "Dress You Up"
    Time: 3:58
    Writers: Peggy Stanziale and Andrea LaRusso
    Producer: Nile Rodgers
    Engineers: Jason Corsaro, with Rob Eaton
  "Shoo-Bee-Doo"
    Time: 5:14
    Writer: Madonna
    Producer: Nile Rodgers
    Engineers: Jason Corsaro, with Rob Eaton
  "Pretender"
    Time: 4:28
    Writers: Madonna and Steve Bray
    Producer: Nile Rodgers
    Engineers: Jason Corsaro, with Rob Eaton
  "Stay"
    Time: 4:04
    Writers: Madonna and Steve Bray
    Producer: Nile Rodgers
    Engineers: Jason Corsaro, with Rob Eaton

Madonna is also featured on the following albums:

"Wotupski!?!" by Jellybean (EMI America Records
  MLP-19011)
Release date: May 1984
  Side One/Cut Two:
    "Sidewalk Talk" by Jellybean, with Madonna
      Time: 6:06
      Writer: Madonna
      Producer: John "Jellybean" Benitez

Vocal Arranger: Madonna
Musical Arrangers: Stephen Bray and Jellybean
Lead Vocal: Catherine Buchanan
Background Vocals: Madonna, Audrey Wheeler,
                  and Cindy Mizelle

"Revenge Of The Killer B's, Volume 2" (Warner
  Bros. Records 1-25068)
Release date: October 1984

Side Two/Cut Five:
"Ain't No Big Deal" by Madonna
  Time: 4:12
  Writer: Stephen Bray
  Producer: Reggie Lucas
  Engineer: Jim Dougherty

Vision Quest Motion Picture Soundtrack (Geffen Records GHS 24063
Release date: February 1985

Side One/Cut Four:
  "Gambler" by Madonna
    Time: 3:54
    Writer: Madonna
    Producer: John "Jellybean" Benitez
    Arranger: Stephen Bray

Side Two/Cut Five
  "Crazy For You" by Madonna
    Time: 4:08

Writers: John Bettis and Jon Lind
Producer: John "Jellybean" Benitez
Arranger: Rob Mounsey

From the soundtrack of the 1985 Orion film *Desperately Seeking Susan*, Madonna performs:

"Into the Groove"
Writers: Madonna and Steve Bray
Producer: John "Jellybean" Benitz
Courtesy of Sire and Warner Brothers Records

12" DISCO SINGLES:

"Everybody" (Sire Records 0-29899), "A" Side
  Release date: 1982
      Time: 5:56
      Writer: Madonna
      Producer: Mark Kamins
      Engineer: Butch Jones
"Everybody" (dubbed version) (Sire Records
  9-29899), "B" Side
  Time: 9:23
  Writer: Madonna
  Producer: Mark Kamins
  Engineer: Butch Jones

"Burning Up" (Sire Records 0-29715), "fast side"
  Release date: 1983
      Time: 5:56
      Writer: Madonna
      Producer: Reggie Lucas
      Engineer: Jim Dougherty
"Physical Attraction" (Sire Records 0-29715), "slow
    side"
      Time: 6:35
      Writer: Reggie Lucas
      Producer: Reggie Lucas
      Engineer: Jim Dougherty
      Remixed by: John "Jellybean" Benitez

  "Holiday" (Sire Records W-9405-T), Side 1
  Note: Available in British pressing only.
  Release Date: 1983

Time: 6:08
Writers: Curtis Hudson and Lisa Stevens
Producer: John ''Jellybean'' Benitez
Engineer: Michael Hutchinson
''Think of Me'' (Sire Records W-9405-T), Side 2
    Time: 4:56
    Writer: Madonna
    Producer: Reggie Lucas
    Engineer: Jim Dougherty

''Borderline'' (Sire Records 020212), Side 1
  Note: This is a totally different production from
        LP version.
  Release Date: 1983
  Time: 6:54
  Writer: Reggie Lucas
  Producers: Reggie Lucas and John ''Jellybean''
  Benitez
  Mixed by: John ''Jellybean'' Benitez
  Mixing Engineer: Michael Hutchinson
''Lucky Star'' (Sire Records 020212) Side 2
  Note: This is a totally different production from
        LP version.
  Time: 7:13
  Writer: Madonna
  Producers: Reggie Lucas and John ''Jellybean''
  Benitez
  Mixed by: John ''Jellybean'' Benitez
  Mixing Engineer: Michael Hutchinson

''Like a Virgin'' (Sire Records 0-20239), Side 1
  Release date: November 1984
  Note: Extended dance remix.

Time: 6:07
Writers: Billy Steinberg and Tom Kelly
Producer: Nile Rodgers
Remixed by: John "Jellybean" Benitez
Remix Engineer: Michael Hutchinson
Assistant Engineer: Melanie West
"Stay" (Sire Records 0-20239), Side 2
Time: 4:04
Writers: Madonna and Steve Bray
Producer: Nile Rodgers
Engineers: Jason Corsaro, with Rob Eaton

"Material Girl" (Sire Records 0-20304), Side 1
Release date: February 1985
Note: Extended dance remix.
Time: 6:06
Writers: Peter Brown and Robert Rans
Producer: Nile Rodgers
Remixed by: John "Jellybean" Benitez
"Pretender" (Sire Records 0-20304), Side 2
Time: 4:28
Writers: Madonna and Steve Bray
Producer: Nile Rodgers
Engineers: Jason Corsaro, with Rob Eaton

SINGLES:

"Everybody" (1982, Sire Records)
"Burning Up" (1983, Sire Records)
"Holiday" (1983, Sire Records)
"Borderline" (1984, Sire Records)
"Lucky Star" (1984, Sire Records)
"Like A Virgin" (1984, Sire Records) † *
"Material Girl" (1985, Sire Records)
"Crazy For You" (1985, Geffen Records)
"Dress You Up" (1985, Sire Records)

†   Certified gold for U.S. sales of 1,000,000.
*   Certified platinum for U.S. sales of 2,000,000.

VIDEOS:

"Everybody" (1982)
   Director: Ed Steinberg
   Note: This is a rarely seen stage video that was
         taped at the New York dance club Paradise
         Garage (not commercially available).

"Burning Up" (1983)*
   Producer: Simon Fields for Limelight Productions
   Director: Steve Baron
   Cinematographer: King Baggot
   Art Director: Julie Towery
   Stylist: Maripol

"Borderline" (1984)*
   Producer: Bruce Logan and Michele Ferrone for
             Bruce Logan, Inc.
   Director: Mary Lambert
   Cinematographer: Andrea Dietrich
   Art Director: Simon Maskell

"Lucky Star" (1984)*
   Producer: Glenn Goodwin for Faultline Films
   Director: Arthur Pierson
   Cinematographer: Wayne Isham

* Available on the commercial video cassette "Madonna"
(Warner Music Video 38101-3).

Art Director: Madonna
Music remixer: John "Jellybean" Benitez

"Like A Virgin" (1984)*
Producer: Simon Fields for Limelight Productions
Director: Mary Lambert
Cinematographer: Peter Sinclair
Art Director: John Ebden
Stylist: Maripol

"Material Girl" (1985)
Producer: Simon Fields for Limelight Productions
Director: Mary Lambert
Cinematographer: Peter Sinclair

"Gambler" (1985), and
"Crazy For You" (1985)
Note: These are both promotional clips from
footage taken for the film *Vision Quest*,
with Madonna singing onstage.

* Available on the commercial video cassette "Madonna"
(Warner Music Video 38101-3).

MOVIES:

A Certain Sacrifice (1984, Cine Cine Productions)
    Note: This is a low-budget experimental film shot between 1979 and 1981. It is not in general release at this time, but may turn up on video cassette or television.

Director: Stephen Jon Lewicki
Producer: Stephen Jon Lewicki
FOR FURTHER INFORMATION about this film, write to:

            Cine Cine Productions
            155 West 81st Street
            Suite 6C
            New York City 10024

"Vision Quest" (1985, Warner Brothers Pictures)
    Note: Madonna only briefly makes a "special appearance" in a club scene.

Director: Harold Becker
Producers: Jon Peters and Peter Guber

Desperately Seeking Susan (1985, Orion Pictures)
    Note: This marks Madonna's professional film debut in an acting role.

Director: Susan Seidelman
Executive Producer: Michael Peyser
Producers: Midge Sanford and Sarah Pillsbury
Production Designer: Santo Loquasto
Screenplay: Leora Barish
Director of Photography: Edward Lachman

About the Author

Mark Bego is the author of two consecutive bestsellers, *Michael!* (Pinnacle Books, 1984) and *On the Road With Michael!* (Pinnacle Books, 1985), which have each sold more than three million copies and have been translated into six languages.

He is the author of three other published books and is currently the Editor-in-Chief of the oldest and most famous show business fan magazine in existence: *Modern Screen*.

Mark has appeared regularly on television as an entertainment reporter and as host of his own talk show. He has produced two stage shows in New York City and has appeared in two feature films.

A native of Detroit, Michigan, Mark Bego currently lives in New York.